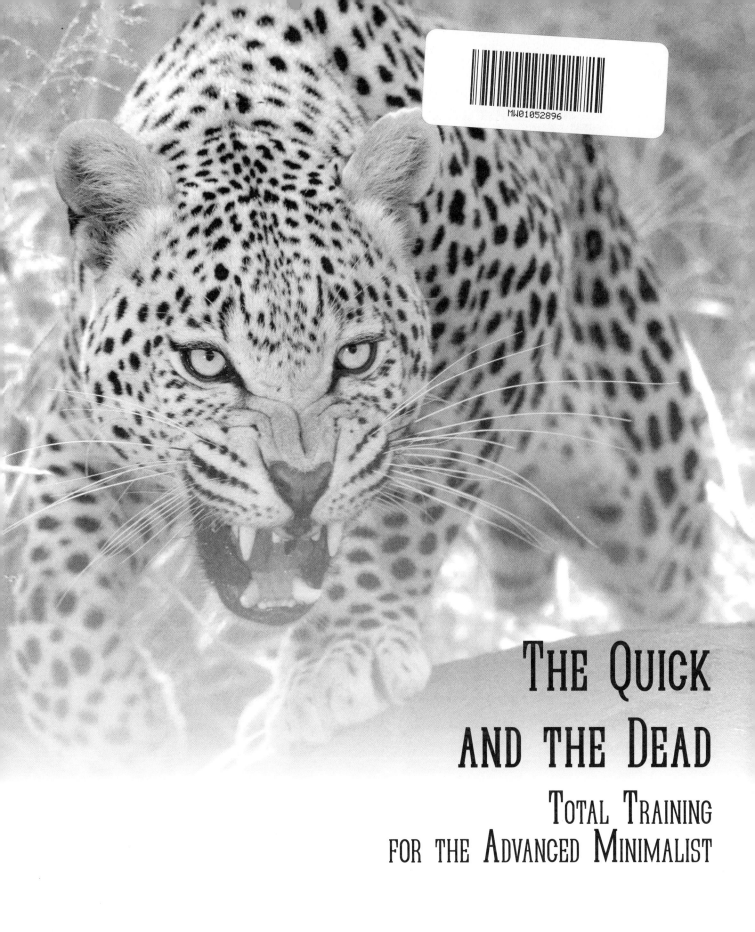

THE QUICK
AND THE DEAD
TOTAL TRAINING
FOR THE ADVANCED MINIMALIST

BY PAVEL

Published by StrongFirst, Inc.

9190 Double Diamond Parkway

Reno, NV 89521, USA

StrongFirst.com

Editor: Laree Draper • www.otpbooks.com

Design: Rachel Darvas • rachel.darvas.sfg@gmail.com

Photography: David Stocco • dlabphotography@gmail.com

Leopard cover photo: Stuart G Porter/Shutterstock.com

Library of Congress Cataloging-in-Publication Data

Tsatsouline, Pavel.

The Quick and the Dead: Total Training for the Advanced Minimalist

ISBN 978-0-9898924-2-1

1. Strength training. 2. Fitness. 3. Physical education and training.

Printed in the United States of America

DISCLAIMER

The author and publisher of this book are not responsible in any manner whatsoever for any injury that may occur through following the instructions contained in this material. The activities may be too strenuous or dangerous for some people. The readers should always consult a physician before engaging in them.

PROLOGUE: The Tale of Two Leopards   5

PART I: FAST FIRST   6

Earn Your Leopard Spots   7

Fast First   11

Acid, the Enemy of the Quick   14

Adrenaline, the Hormone of Prey   18

The Quick and the Dead   21

PART II: THE FEROCITY OF LIFE   23

A Long and Winding Road   24

The Three Energy Systems   26

The Emergency System   27

Intensity Is Not the Effort but the Output 28

...And Then the Wheels Come Off   30

Sweet Spot in Time   31

Fast 10s—an Explosive Equal of Heavy Fives 34

10x10, Reloaded   35

The Melody Is in the Rests   37

A Rugby Lesson   39

The Finishing Touches   40

PART III: THE POWER DRILLS   44

The Power Drills of Choice   45

The Swing: Violent as a Hunt in the Savannah 55

The Pushup: A Classic, Remastered   59

The Snatch: Hail Tsar!   68

PART IV: HAPPY HUNTING!   72

Circuit Training, Limited   73

Where Is the Cardio?   76

The Delta 20 Principle   78

Built to Last   82

The Schedule   84

Q&D Summary: Swings and Pushups   86

Q&D Summary: Snatches   88

Each Chooses for Oneself   91

EPILOGUE: Animal Supreme   97

Acknowledgements   98

References and Notes   98

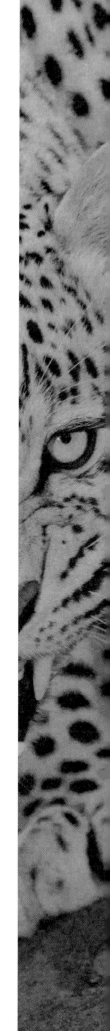

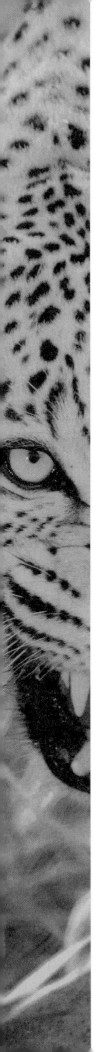

To KT

Prologue: The Tale of Two Leopards

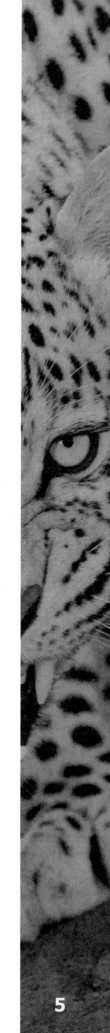

The antelope was grazing, oblivious of the superbly camouflaged cat stealthily closing in. The predator flowed like mercury, hugging the terrain.

It was a busy day in the savannah, but only one pair of eyes was tracking the leopard. My friend George had put in his time in Africa fighting poachers and he knew how to see without being seen. Recently he had been entertaining himself timing big cats' hunts.

The blurry spot in the tall grass became a straw-colored streak. The antelope made a desperate run for its life, a run that was blissfully short. The *panthera* leaped. Her jaws, powerful enough to crush thick bones, closed on her prey's neck.

It was over in 16 seconds. The proud hunter stood tall, surveyed her surroundings the way a big boss would, and made a brief "fast and loose" victory dance. Then she picked up her dinner, which was bigger than herself, and climbed a tree with it.

"It would be like you climbing a tree holding me in your teeth," commented George, who has good 50 pounds on me. And that was no feat for a leopard that can climb with carcasses three times her bodyweight.

Then George told me of another leopard hunt he had witnessed, very different from the first.

The male cat did not have it easy. Age was taking its toll and one of his front paws was infected. A thorn was wedged in it, a common hazard to alpha predators in the wild.

He also made his kill, but, as he was slower, he had to work harder and longer to bring the antelope down. Then he was unable to get to a tree fast enough to stash his cat food—and was attacked by a pack of opportunistic hyenas.

The tom fought hard and well and the hyenas ran off with their tails between their legs. George stopped his timer at four minutes.

Luckily, the hyenas did not return. Exhausted, the old tom lay panting on the ground. Can you even imagine a cat panting? It is below the dignity of a cat.

Finally, the old leopard got his bad breath back and dragged his dinner to the safety of a tree.

A few months later, George watched the same leopard retire to a cave to die. That is what they do.

PART I: FAST FIRST

Earn Your Leopard Spots

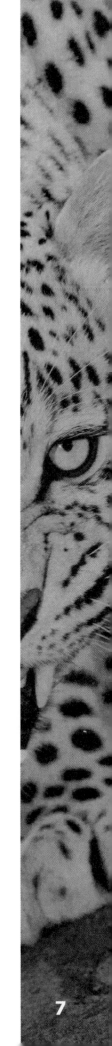

The second leopard hunt exemplifies the mentality of today's "high intensity interval training." Dramatic, inefficient, costly. I admire the old cat's tough style, given his circumstances of age taking its toll—but his heroics are not something to emulate on a Wednesday night at the gym.

In contrast, the Quick and the Dead regimen (Q&D) was inspired by the first cat. Not a single set exceeds the duration of her ferocious 16-second kill. Power undiluted by fatigue is not heroic; it is professional.

The Q&D protocol was designed to maximize your performance at a lowest biological cost—and to leave you fresh and able to perform at a high level, physically and mentally, at any time.

You will get powerful. Very powerful.

While power is awesome for its own sake, training it in a particular manner also delivers a wide range of "what the hell effects." Muscle hypertrophy. Fat loss. Endurance. Anti-fragility. Anti-aging.

Plus, Q&D will enable you to make greater strength gains if you are also lifting.

Q&D can be a minimalist's stand-alone, total training method.

Or make a quality addition to any athlete's regimen.

Q&D does not beat up the body and takes only 12–30 minutes per training session, two to three times per week.

Q&D was designed to minimize detraining when circumstances force you to lay off or cut back. If you get a hare-brained idea to take an entire month off all training and then go back to your boxing class and pretend you never left, you will suffer less than expected.

A US special operator I will call "Mark" is an accomplished boxer, wrestler, and powerlifter. His strength has enabled him to stay in the fight into his mid-40s. Then he added a Q&D swing and pushup plan to his training—back when it was called "StrongFirst Experimental Protocol 033."

I have completed the six-week 033C template. I did it as a warm-up for my powerlifts three days a week, always for 30 minutes. I noticed a speed increase in all my powerlifts and pain relief of all of my injuries.

I also found an increase in endurance while doing combatives. And as my hips developed more explosive movement, my speed came up, creating increased striking power. The big game changer I noticed was my hip movement in grappling. I am able to maximize force through explosive hip movement, coincidentally making me less tired.

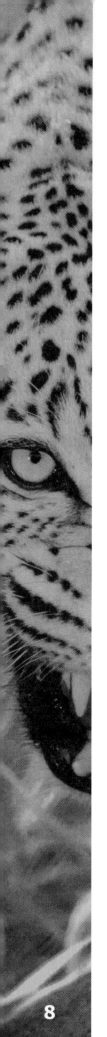

I am more efficient with energy by driving my hips and getting "heavy" on my opponent. Combining that force with leverage has me launching big dudes like children. By getting my hips under and driving up versus using my arms and back during takedowns and throws has made me more efficient and explosive.

Also, I am more cognizant of my breathing. I am using more "breath behind the shield" [1] as I roll versus using the more traditional skip breathing. I am less hypoxic and have better clarity of my opponent's body position and movements.

I lost nine pounds and, based on my visual composition, I would say it was fat loss. I gave up sugar at the same time, so I would say it is a combination of factors. My arms have definitely gotten bigger.

Overall, I found the 033C enjoyable and meditative. I was able to go into a flow state and felt I could go on forever. After not touching a kettlebell in a few years, I felt this was a great way to get things going again.

I need to get a larger kettlebell!

Q&D is every bit as applicable to the female of the species as it is to the male.

Did you know that in a lion pride, it is the lionesses that do most of the hunting?

I come from a culture with strong women. They fought alongside the men in World War II, making history as snipers and pilots. My grand aunt was a highly decorated vet. She was in her third year of med school when the Nazis invaded. Young Natasha joined up and spent the four years of the Great War on the front line as a nurse. When she returned home after the war and finished her education, she became a civilian aviation doctor. A majority of doctors in the Soviet Union were women, by the way.

On a lighter side, a Russian wife asks her husband, "Do you love me?" He answers, "Not only do I love you; I also respect and slightly fear you."

---

[1] "Breathing behind the shield" is taught in *Kettlebell Simple & Sinister.*

Other than opening doors for them, at StrongFirst we do not treat women any differently than men. We do not disrespect them with any nonsense about "long, lean muscle" or "shaping the female problem areas." So when Italian athlete Ilaria Scopece, SFG/SFB, approached Fabio Zonin for training advice while preparing for an important competition, the Master SFG gave her the same 033 plan that became Q&D.

Ilaria weighs as much as a 48kg Beast kettlebell—only she is a lot more dangerous. Scopece is the number-one ranked professional light flyweight boxer in Europe.

Starting with 15 reps in the 30-second timed test with a 20kg kettlebell in the one-arm hard style swing, in a few months Ilaria did 21 reps. That 40-percent increase would have been notable on its own, but the fighter did it with 24kg—a 20-percent weight increase.

Ilaria Scopece, the number-one ranked professional light flyweight boxer in Europe and a StrongFirst certified instructor

Ilaria's performance is identical to that of a 200-pound man doing 21 crisp and perfect one-arm swings with a 48kg Beast in 30 seconds.

Where in the pre-test she lifted 300 pounds of iron in half a minute, in the post-test the lady put up over 500. For perspective, her performance is identical to that of a 200-pound man doing 21 crisp and perfect one-arm swings in 30 seconds with a Beast.

But kettlebells do not strike back. Ilaria's performance in the ring is far more important than her swing and pushup numbers. Her boxing coach put her through a test: 10 rounds, alternating between two experienced sparring partners, both 15-percent heavier than her.

"While sparring with my partners, I realized I had even greater speed and explosiveness and I was able to maintain this for the whole match…I had gas to sell."

In her next fight, Ilaria knocked out her opponent from Eastern Europe 37 seconds into the first round.

We have many great stories like these.

But The Quick and the Dead is not for everyone.

Q&D is not for beginners. When we tested various experimental plans, we discovered that while everyone improved on Q&D, to our great surprise, experienced athletes improved the most. Fighters, military special operators, professional baseball players, motocross riders, and guys who could press the Beast for reps made much more dramatic progress—in both absolute and relative terms—than ladies and gents who were still working their way up to the Simple standard of *Kettlebell Simple & Sinister*.

While this should not make any sense, we concluded there were good reasons for this paradox.

First, Q&D training demands a foundation of strength. Without a rock-solid midsection that comes from paying dues to heavy metal or high tension, there is no way of expressing one's max power. As Dr. Fred Hatfield quipped decades ago, "You cannot shoot a cannon from a canoe."

KETTLEBELL
SIMPLE & SINISTER
BY PAVEL

Second, power is a learned skill. A low-level athlete seems to need the artificial resistance of muscle congestion to exert against. He or she is unable to just explode against a moderate weight. As a result, a relative beginner lacks the intensity needed to produce the desired metabolic events, finds the Q&D protocol ridiculously easy, and only nets a partial adaptation. S&S, which on the power-to-acid continuum lies somewhere between Q&D and HIIT, is the perfect program for this athlete.

Finally, it is a matter of personality. While some individuals are "cats," most are "dogs" or "persistence hunters." Solitary cats are masters of brief and explosive bursts; persistence hunters wear their prey down. Dogs feel the burn somewhere in between.

That said, even if you are not a "natural cat," you have a lot to gain from training like one—at least as your secondary modality. We have seen high-level athletes get excellent results from adding Q&D to their endurance training.

In addition to watching out for your health, Q&D will improve the quality of your life.

"Metcons" ravage your system with acid, free radicals, and toxic ammonia. They deplete your muscles' energy pool in a manner similar to chronic fatigue syndrome and leave your carcass sore, tired, and injury prone. They burn you out mentally, wreak havoc with your hormones, and make you feel like hell. Are you willing to pay such a high price for getting "in shape"?

And if you are, say, a first responder, is it fair to the citizens you will be saving?

FAST FIRST

You can be anything you want. A warrior. An athlete. A hard man or woman ready to handle whatever life throws at you. But you must be strong first.

Once you are strong—even kind of strong—consider shifting your focus to power.

$P = F \times v$

Power equals force multiplied by velocity. It demands a precise blend of strength and speed.

Why should you train power?

First, for its own sake. Being powerful is awesome.

Second, for an impressive array of "what the hell effects" (WTHEs) that come with it.

As demonstrated by science and experience, an advanced minimalist will substantially improve in all key fitness components by power-centric training. And a serious athlete will spike performance in any sport, while reducing the total amount of training.

High-level Soviet athletes from different sports were subjected to a battery of tests of different qualities. As expected, most severely lagged in attributes outside their specialties: Weightlifters and gymnasts had no endurance and endurance athletes no strength. Sprinters were outliers who stood out with their all-around development; their strength was not far behind that of strength athletes, plus they had respectable endurance.

Having compared what training foci on different attributes—speed, power, strength, and endurance—can do for other qualities, renowned biochemist Prof. Nikolay Yakovlev concluded that:

> The most multipurpose loads are speed and power. They trigger biochemical changes that are a foundation of not only speed but also of strength and endurance...Strength loads create biochemical preconditions for the development of not only strength but, to some degree, speed...Prolonged steady state loads develop only endurance for extended work.

Yakovlev collected fascinating data comparing the effects of these different types of training on muscles. It revealed what pure power training can do for all-around fitness. Take a look at some of the good professor's numbers.

Hypertrophy			
Exercises			
Endurance	Sprint	Power	Strength
Myosin—% improvement from untrained levels			
0	18	60	59

Myosin is a contractile protein, the "piston" part of the muscle cell that moves and produces force. The above numbers declare that quick lifts can build muscle just as well as "grinds." And they do it with much lighter weights: Max power is expressed at a third to a half of maximal strength[2] and is typically trained with resistance just slightly heavier than that. Do not be surprised that such light weights stimulate fast fibers; the faster the movement, the less force it takes to recruit them.

When it comes to hypertrophy, we cannot ignore testosterone. Although we know a lot less about the influence of different hormones on body composition than pop fitness publications would have us believe and even less about the effects of different types of exercise on the endocrine system, it is well established that increasing testosterone by hook or by crook helps build muscle. A number of studies have shown testosterone shooting up in the aftermath of power exercise, for instance over 15 percent after five sets of 10 light jump squats. Scientists generally agree that, "High power resistance exercise protocols…produce acute increases of testosterone… [that] may partially explain the muscle hypertrophy observed in athletes who routinely employ high power resistance exercise."

A student doing jump squats at a Strong Endurance™ seminar

---

[2] "Maximal strength" is not always synonymous with "1RM." It may be true in the bench press but not the squat. Factor in the *system mass*: everything you are lifting, including your own carcass. In many exercises, such as kettlebell swings or sprint accelerations, max strength cannot be measured at all.

Power training is also a key to staying young; testosterone is only a part of that picture.

As we age, speed goes first, strength next, and endurance last. Prof. Yakovlev pointed out that you will never see a 70-year-old burning rubber on a 100-meter sprint, while countless folks of the same vintage casually cover 15–20k while hunting or picking mushrooms. As for strength, its dynamic component declines first (jumps, throws, quick lifts), while static and slow strength stick around much longer.

In aging, there is a preferential loss of type II fibers; a sedentary 80-year-old man has lost half the fast fibers he had as a 30-year-old. Even grandmas and grandpas whose lifestyles do not involve anything more dynamic than bingo should be concerned. "The ability of muscles to produce force rapidly is vital and may serve as a protective mechanism when falling," emphasize Profs. Vladimir Zatsiorsky and William Kraemer. They add that while this decline cannot be prevented, it looks like it can be reduced with power training, as witnessed by performances of master power and strength athletes.

With age, the intensity of oxidative processes also decreases. At rest and per pound, 70-year-olds consume 40 percent less oxygen than 20- and 30-year-olds, with a resulting reduction in work capacity.

A World War II vet not prone to babying himself or others, Prof. Yakovlev prescribed accelerations as the number one exercise choice for the elderly to stimulate both the plastic and the energetic processes (in other words, muscle building and aerobic). Beefing up one's mitochondria and fast-twitch fibers with power training is a great prescription for turning back the clock.

On to endurance.

Aerobic Power			
Exercises			
Endurance	Sprint	Power	Strength
Maximal tissue respiration rate— % improvement from untrained levels			
53	45	48	20

The *maximal tissue respiration rate* refers to the amount of traffic one's aerobic power plants, the *mitochondria*, can handle. Naturally, dedicated endurance training was first—but power came in a very close second.

This is especially awesome once you consider that these stamina gains were "free"—made without sucking wind or muscle "burn."

Sprinting is nothing like "high intensity interval training;" it is ultra-short dashes with decadent rest periods. Legendary Canadian sprint coach Charlie Francis had his athletes start with a 15-minute rest after the first sub-eight-second sprint and increased the rests from there. Power training is not "metcon," but sets of low reps with generous breaks—at least two to five minutes.

In summary, with fatigue being the antithesis of power training, the endurance adaptations the latter produces are pure WTHEs. Moreover, once you arrange these power sets in a special manner to maximize mitochondrial adaptation, as we will do later in the book, they will be a game changer for your conditioning.

David Rigert at his "dry fighting weight"

From the fat loss perspective, scientists conclude that speed training improves aerobic oxidation of carbs but not of fats. Nevertheless, per Prof. Vladimir Platonov, "When training at high speeds, there is a greater decrease in fatty tissue as compared to training at low speeds." I could drone on about improved insulin sensitivity, but since it would bore me out of my skull, I will not.

At StrongFirst, we never focus on fat loss—and get it anyway as a side effect of our strength and power pursuits. Geoff Neupert, a former Master SFG instructor and an accomplished Olympic weightlifter, points out how lean weightlifters are, all without the dishonor of aerobics. Indeed, the Soviet national team had a standard of six- to seven-percent body fat for everyone but the heavyweights—David Rigert, one of the greatest weightlifters of all time, had four-percent body fat at a bodyweight of 200–220. He called it a "dry fighting weight."

Of course, eating clean helped. Here is Rigert's typical breakfast: two raw eggs, two steaks with no side dishes, almost half a pound of sour cream, a cup of coffee, and mineral water.

ACID, THE ENEMY OF THE QUICK

Over 200 years ago, Swedish scientist Jöns Berzelius discovered lactic acid in the muscles of an exhausted stag that had just been hunted down.

Acid is the enemy of both tension and relaxation, drawing one into the stiff no-man's land in between. It muffles the brain's commands to the muscles, inhibits all three energy systems, and interferes with contraction and relaxation—read: strength and speed—in many ways.

As your speed goes down, you are moving to the right on the quick–dead continuum.

Max Dedik, Kyokushin karate champion and accomplished coach, is an enemy of metcons for fighters: "I often see prescriptions like 50 or 100 burpees in one or two sets. Go ahead, do it, but you will definitely lose speed."

Dedik suggests comparing the speed exhibited during tournaments in full contact styles, like his own, and noncontact ones. "Point fighters avoid significant acidosis in training, as they know it ruins speed. And speed is their end-all...Compare the speed of their champions and ours. Any questions?"

Both speed and strength take a dive in acid, but power suffers the most. In fatigued muscles, speed and strength decrease by a similar percentage. This compounds the power drop-off, since power is an offspring of both. For instance, if the force and the velocity each go down by 20 percent, the power will tank by 40 percent. Feel free to add an exclamation mark.

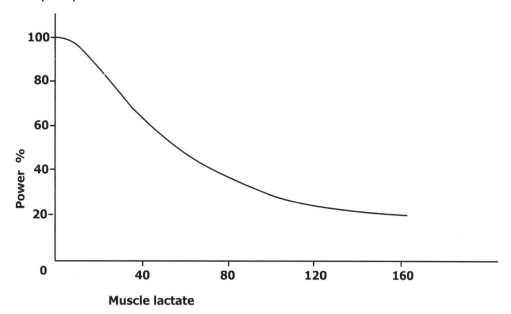

Correlation between lactate concentration in the working muscles and the power output

When your burst of effort is any longer than the magnificent first cat's hunt or if your rests are too brief—as in HIIT or metcons—power goes down. Way down. For instance, by the end of an all-out 30-second bicycle or velo sprint, power drops by up to 50 percent.

Contemplate that: In just half a minute, acid cuts your power in half.

No longer able to contract quickly and powerfully, fatigued muscles compensate with longer and weaker contractions. This messes up movement coordination. It could mean failing to catch dinner—or becoming dinner yourself. Even if you have avoided such a fate, you are learning slowness and poor form for the next time.

Accustomed to always pushing through a sticky mud of muscle congestion, an athlete develops a particular movement stereotype. His allegedly explosive movements are anything but—as exemplified by burpees in metcon gyms. Sensei Dedik has seen it time and again: Fighters who abuse metcons lose speed and sharpness in their strikes. Instead of practicing to be quick, they are practicing to be dead.

Even if you survived your HIIT session today, you might become dinner tomorrow or the day after, drained of energy and crippled by soreness.

Old-school coaches knew what they were talking about: Lactic acid makes you sore. Today's consensus is it is the fault of the microtrauma caused by eccentric contractions. Without questioning the latter, I insist that the former is just as guilty.

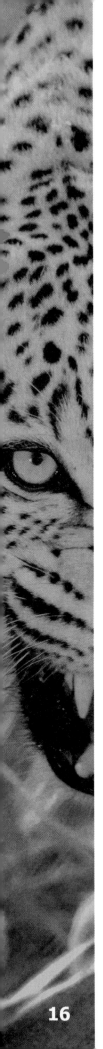

Conduct an experiment. Leaf through your training log and find some less-than-brilliant workout that made you very sore. Say, you did as many pushups as you could, rested for a minute, did it again, and then a third time. Recall how your shoulders and triceps felt for days.

Now, match the number of pushups, using the identical technique—but spread them throughout the day into sets of five reps done every 15 minutes.

After a couple of days of feeling great, you will never roll your eyes at an old-timer with a whistle and a stopwatch telling you that lactic acid makes you sore.

The acid does not literally burn holes through your muscles—but it triggers various processes that do.

Within your muscles are tiny bubbles, *lysosomes*, containing enzymes that dismantle and dispose of the components that are damaged or no longer needed. Lysosomes operate exclusively in an acidic environment. When acidity is moderate, they do what they are supposed to do, and even help muscles grow. But when the "burn" is out of control, lysosomes go on a destructive rampage that you feel a day or two after.

"We want—in sports and health training—to develop and renew cells, while some defective structures need to be destroyed," comments Prof. Victor Selouyanov. "The 'game' is a slight acidosis to enable the cell to renew but not self-destruct. Overly active lysosomes can lead to cellular death."

Although some lactic acid is needed to promote muscle hypertrophy through several mechanisms that are outside the scope of this book, its excess is destructive. Russians did a study to evaluate the anabolic and catabolic effects of different types of exercises and loads. Among those tested was a typical HIIT workout, 3x60 seconds on a veloergometer with two-minute rests. It was the most catabolic of all types of exercise; the anabolic phase was not reached even on day four.

To put things into perspective, another one of the tested loads was 10 sets of 20 frog jumps. This was also very catabolic—but less than the one before, in spite of the severe eccentric loading! And the anabolic phase finally did kick in after two or three days. These results are even more striking once we learn that the subjects were speedskaters—athletes accustomed to metcons, but not to eccentric loading.

Another way acid contributes to tissue damage and soreness is by stimulating the production of free radicals or *reactive oxygen species* (ROS).

Like lactic acid, in moderate quantities free radicals perform many useful functions. In excess, they destroy performance, health, and life itself. The dose makes the poison.

Metcons are custom made for maximizing ROS generation. You may have heard of *glutathione* (GSH), "the mother of all antioxidants" produced by our bodies. Scientists measure the concentrations of its "used up" version to assess oxidative stress. They found a linear relationship between its concentration and lactate concentration after exhaustive exercise.

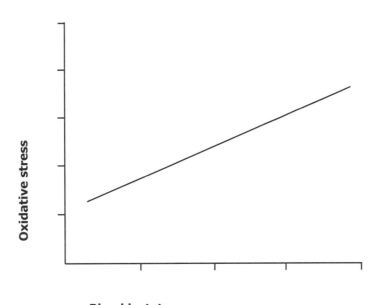

A linear relationship between lactate concentration and oxidative stress

Leading researcher Prof. Maya Pshennikova concluded that ROS are a major destructive factor of various muscle fiber structures. It has been suggested by other Russian specialists that free radical hyper production in soft and connective tissues may cause degenerative changes and a loss of elasticity leading to injuries. It is very likely that by breaking your acid habit and implementing Q&D protocols, you will improve the quality of your soft tissues. This is what Peter Park, a strength and conditioning coach of champions, keeps hearing from the therapists who do bodywork on his elite athletes from a variety of sports. And this is one of the many reasons Q&D is a perfect choice for those whom Senior SFG instructor Alexey Senart calls "older model Terminators."

Leave metcons, exhaustion, stiffness, and soreness to prey. Stay fresh to hunt another day.

Peter Park coaching JJ Muno

Speaks Peter Park, strength and conditioning coach of Giancarlo Stanton, Lance Armstrong, Justin Verlander, Ken Roczen, Diana Taurasi, and other high-level athletes:

> *I train the entire spectrum of the population, ranging from professional baseball and football players, motocross riders, cyclists, triathletes, golfers to high-end CEOs and high school athletes. I have not only seen incredible "what the hell" results with Pavel's Quick and the Dead, everyone I work with reports better energy, great recovery, and improved body composition. In this book, Pavel reveals a minimalist program that will benefit any human.*

ADRENALINE, THE HORMONE OF PREY

"…the blank serenity of the invulnerable."

Novelist Peter Benchley's depiction of a barracuda is a good lesson in how to approach your training. An impassive face. Violent power without psyching.

Prey is stressed. Predators are not.

Stress and adrenaline exacerbate the free radical damage initiated by lactic acid. Welcome to the "high intensity interval training" class! Amateurish treatment of every workout as a competition—often jacked up on some "energy drink"—makes the bad worse.

Damage caused by ROS intensifies during stress, regardless of the nature of the stress. And adrenaline bridges the physical and the psychological causes of the metcon-induced oxidative damage. This hormone inhibits synthesis of the earlier-mentioned antioxidant GSH—and a high concentration of adrenaline almost doubles the mitochondrial damage by free radicals. The body is efficient; if you are about to become lunch, why worry about accelerated aging?

Both adrenaline and noradrenaline are mobilizing hormones, but their effects are different and their ratio varies among individuals and species. Adrenaline appears to be associated with fear and noradrenaline with aggression. In case you believe that going full "Sparta" is hardcore, consider the following:

Adrenaline-to-Noradrenaline Ratios in Different Species

Rabbit	50:1
Chicken	10:1
Human	5:1
Lion	1:1

Which do you aspire to be?

Should you argue that "everyone psyches up for their workouts," know that baboons and other social animals prone to peer pressure also have a high adrenaline-to-noradrenaline ratio—just like rabbits.

But what about world-class powerlifters? Don't they work themselves into an adrenaline frenzy?

Lions on the platform: Dan Austin and Hideaki Inaba. Austin's world deadlift record, 705.5 pounds at a bodyweight of 148 pounds set in 1992, is still untouchable over a quarter of a century later.

Yes—twice a year, at the Nationals and the Worlds. They know that the rabbit is more motivated than the lion and it is worth acting like you are fighting for your life when a title or a record is at stake. These lifters also know that once they have used up their adrenaline charge on the competition platform, they will be walking dead for three weeks. So, the remaining 350 days of the year, they spare the rabbit hormone and stay in the lion mode when training: focused and not hyped.

An aside that will appeal to the well-rounded reader: A creative high that increases physical and mental work capacity is accompanied by noradrenaline secretion. Perhaps this explains why the samurai were equally proficient at war and poetry.

Noradrenaline also appears to be secreted in situations with a certain outcome, and adrenaline in uncertainty and anxiety. Not surprisingly, whales beat even lions in their noradrenaline prevalence—no threats or uncertainties for them. Ditto for elite lifters. They know exactly how many reps they are going to do. There is no doubt and no possibility of failure. Throughout an extraordinary career that spanned decades and over a hundred world records, Ed Coan never missed a rep in training! Always calm and unperturbed, you could swear Ed got Botox.

The powerful are skilled at relaxing. Did you know that leopards purr like house cats?

THE QUICK AND THE DEAD

In the South American jungle, a jaguar hunts a prey that bites back, a caiman. In a show of absolute superiority, the cat makes his kill on the dangerous dinner's turf. The jag jumps into the river and snatches the wriggling toothy reptile by its neck.

A caiman or a gator may be fast, but if he misses, he is in deep trouble, as he just shot a musket—a single-shot muzzle loader against a warm-blooded predator's six-shooter that can be rapidly reloaded. A reptile's weak aerobic system and reliance on glycolysis puts it at a great disadvantage against warm-blooded predators whose aerobic systems enable them to rapidly recover from their lightning strikes.

A gator needs many hours of rest and sucking wind to clear the acid produced by a single spurt of activity. Scientists believe that dinosaurs—reptiles' cousins—had similar metabolism, which made them vulnerable to mammal predators whose aerobic systems were far superior and that enabled them to sustain their attacks.

Enter the home of the aerobic system, the *mitochondria*, our cells' power plants.

This book did not start out as a power-centric guide to total fitness with a health twist. The original intention was to write only about improving endurance for high-power applications by training the mitochondria.

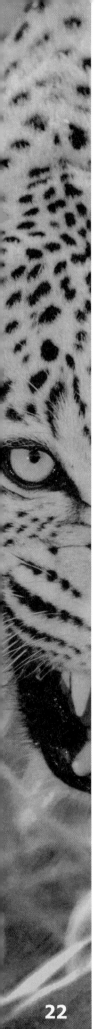

As it turns out, the state of one's mitochondria determines much more than the outcome of a rowing race or a judo match. The mitochondria are, in Dr. Nick Lane's words, "the masters of life and death."

The alternative of being "quick" to being "dead" in the African savannah or the old American West only scratches the surface of the inspiration behind the book's title.

"Who shall give account to Him who is ready to judge the quick and the dead." ~ I Peter 4:5

In the Bible, the word "quick" does not describe being quick on the draw. It means "alive." The goal of the Q&D regimen is not just to get you to perform at a high level, but to do it in a way that does no harm to your health—and hopefully improves it a great deal.

The Old English word "quicken" meant "to come to life." The unborn child's first movement in the womb was called "quickening." Fittingly, we get our mitochondrial genes from our mothers.

Healthy, strong, and abundant mitochondria make one much more resilient to a variety of stressors: cold, heat, altitude, infection, poison, radiation, etc.

On the other hand, mitochondrial dysfunction is a likely cause of cardiovascular and neurodegenerative diseases, cancer, diabetes, obesity, and aging.

Mitochondria are the primary source of free radical generation in our bodies. You can eat blueberries until you are blue in the face, yet they are not going to save you from ROS: Antioxidant foods and supplements have turned out to be surprisingly ineffective. What you need are more, bigger, and better mitochondria. They not only generate and leak fewer free radicals—they act as "net sinks," as Dr. Alexander Andreyev put it.

If you plan on remaining quick—as in "alive"—as long as possible, you had better treat your mitochondria right.

Choices that damage mitochondria include the usual suspects of smoking, drinking, overeating, eating garbage, pollution, and overtraining.

Choices that build mitochondria are caloric restriction, intermittent fasting, controlled hypoxia and hypothermia, and steady-state aerobic training.

Then there is the state of the art training designed to beef up the mitochondria in your fast-twitch fibers: Q&D.

PART II: THE FEROCITY OF LIFE

A Long and Winding Road

Back in the 1980s, the glory days of Soviet sports, Prof. Yuri Verkhoshansky had a revolutionary endurance training idea.

What if instead of training the athlete to tolerate ever-increasing concentrations of lactic acid, we trained him to produce less of it?

Anti-glycolytic training (AGT) was born.

Born in a country that no longer exists, AGT culminated in the 21st century with remarkable performance breakthroughs on a number of Russian national teams in a mind-numbingly diverse array of sports: judo, cross country skiing, rowing, cycling, full-contact karate.

This is how Prof. Verkhoshansky summed up AGT: "…training must have an 'anti-glycolytic' direction, that is, lower glycolysis involvement to an absolute possible minimum."

Thus it was written.

More than five years ago, members of the StrongFirst instructor leadership asked me to develop the next generation of conditioning protocols. I agreed, thinking it would be easy. I intended to apply the existing Soviet and Russian AGT research to kettlebell swings and other exercises in the StrongFirst arsenal. I was certain I could write a book in a couple of months. Little did I know what kind of a rabbit hole I was burrowing down.

Since the primary adaptation target in AGT is the mitochondrion, I decided to do my due diligence and review the literature, both Russian and Western, on mitochondrial adaptation in fast-twitch fibers to exercise. Annoyingly, the two were decidedly at odds.

Prof. Verkhoshansky was an empiricist. He operated with black boxes and usually chose not to mess around under the hood of the cell. His approach was remarkably successful, considering at least two major breakthroughs he contributed to the sports world: "plyometrics" and AGT.

His method also assured that his works would live on. Explanations come and go; results stay. As the old scientist joke goes, "That works very well in practice, but how does it work in theory?"

While Verkhoshansky did not speculate on the biochemical events powering his innovation, his successors did. They hypothesized that by creating aerobic conditions in fast fibers, AGT increases the size and number of mitochondria in them.

Unfortunately, according to some very reliable Western research, this only works in slow fibers.

Shortly after hitting this first wall, I plowed into a second one. Some Russian specialists stated that high acidity destroys mitochondria—while in the US, HIIT was used to build them.

Reconciling these contradictions took me several years and many headaches. Without going into gory details—this is what the Strong Endurance™ seminar is for—this is what I concluded.

Champion martial artist Andżelika Stefańska holds nothing back as she is using fellow SFG Team Leader Mike Sousa as a heavy bag while demonstrating an anti-glycolytic training protocol for fighters at a Strong Endurance™ seminar.

Soviet and Russian AGT, while it somewhat increases the mitochondrial quantity (size and number), is not optimized for it. It excels at enhancing the mitochondrial quality—upgrading the mitochondria to handle heavier traffic and rendering the incoming acid harmless.

HIIT increases both mitochondrial quantity and quality, but in a haphazard way and often at an unacceptably high cost.

Western scientists did a fine job of identifying the cellular pathways leading to mitochondrial biogenesis or creation. They traced the metabolic events triggering these pathways. Other scientists, those who experimented with HIIT, paid token attention to these discoveries and viewed them out of context of the many other biochemical reactions taking place at the same time and some of the events happening in the body at large. The resulting training protocols worked, but often inefficiently and with serious side effects. Like drugs with long disclaimers in small print.

Deep soreness. Low energy. Stress. Hormones out of whack. Free radical damage. Unfavorable changes in the heart.

I became convinced there was a better way.

There is some fairly dense science awaiting you around the corner. Although I explain the madness behind the method in lay terms, I realize that such reading is not everyone's cup of tea. Should you choose to, you may skip half the book and go straight to *Part IV, Happy Hunting*! You big sissy.

THE THREE ENERGY SYSTEMS

I have no intention of boring you with a detailed dissection of the energy systems because you either know this stuff or do not care (in either case, you are welcome). Here are a few highlights relevant to Q&D.

Carbs, fats, and proteins contain energy, which, to use a financial analogy, is not "liquid." Before it is spent by muscles and elsewhere, it needs to be converted into "cash" called *ATP*.

What is "A"? This information is on a need-to-know basis and you do not need to know. Since it is the structure around which ATP is built, we will nickname it the "A-frame."

"P" stands for "phosphate," a molecule containing phosphorus. This element is known for forming chemical bonds loaded with energy and easily releasing them.

"T" means "tri" and refers to the number of phosphate groups attached to the "A-frame."

When ATP is split to release energy, it loses one "P" and becomes *ADP*, where "D" stands for "di," two.

When one goes from zero to 60, the body's ATP demands increase up to 1,000-fold. The problem is, ATP, being a capacitor rather than a battery, drains quickly. Stored ATP can power only a half to one-and-a-half seconds of maximal intensity work. ATP has to be constantly replenished by the so-called *energy systems* that put the missing "P" back in. There are three main energy systems:

- *Creatine phosphate (CP)*
- *Glycolytic*
- *Aerobic*

The following highly generalized diagram represents what happens in a given muscle in an all-out dynamic effort such as a sprint or a set of hard style swings.

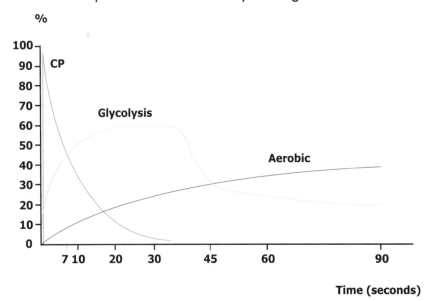

Approximate contribution of the three main energy systems to the total energy output in trained athletes in brief, all-out dynamic exercise

- The CP and aerobic systems are efficient and clean burning. In contrast, on the glycolysis watch, muscles produce acid that rapidly accumulates and creates many problems, both short- and long-term.

- The CP system is one-and-a-half to two times more powerful than the glycolytic system and three or four times more powerful than the aerobic system. The CP system is the one the cat used to earn her dinner.

- The CP system revs up to full power in point-five to point-seven seconds, while glycolysis takes about 20 seconds, and the aerobic system one to four minutes. CP is the rapid deployment force.

- Although it takes about 30 seconds of all-out sprinting to fully exhaust the CP "rocket fuel," the CP system can sustain its max power for only about five seconds and something close to it for eight to 10 seconds, and then rapidly fizzles. It is telling that even the best sprinters slow down toward the end of a 100-meter race.

To clear up this contradiction, consider an analogy. Imagine a car designed by an Orwellian state to never run out of gas. As long as the tank is at least half full, it allows you to put the pedal to the metal. Once the half mark is passed, the cyber nanny starts pinching off the fuel lines. No matter how hard you pump the pedal, the closer the needle edges toward empty, the more sluggish the car becomes. Driven crazy, you will stop to refuel long before this happens, just as the Big Brother intended.

This is exactly how the CP system was designed. The emptier the CP tank gets, the more the throttle is closed. This feature has profound implications on performance and adaptation.

The Emergency System

In the title of *The Three Musketeers*, Alexandre Dumas omitted the fourth member of the crew and the main protagonist, d'Artagnan. Many biochemistry textbooks do the same when they discuss the energy systems. How many readers have heard about the fourth energy system, the *myokinase* system?

When the three main energy pathways are unable to keep up with the demand for ATP, the organism breaks the glass and presses the red button. The fourth musketeer to the rescue! Enter the fourth energy system, *myokinase* (MK), that Prof. Nikolay Yakovlev called the "emergency system." This system is especially active about 10–20 seconds into an all-out dynamic effort, for reasons that will soon become clear.

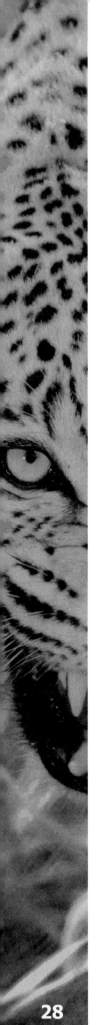

The myokinase system ekes out some energy by breaking off another phosphate group from the "A-frame." The capacitor loses another "stripe" and ADP becomes *AMP*. You may have guessed that "M" stands for "mono" and refers to the last phosphate group standing.

The MK reaction takes a "P" from one ADP molecule and attaches it to another ADP molecule, thus making AMP out of the former and ATP out of the latter:

$$MK$$

$$2\ ADP \leftrightarrows ATP + AMP$$

Now the capacitor is fully drained. Even though on paper AMP still has one phosphate group, it does not store any more energy.

This "fourth musketeer" not only saves your tail at the given instant, it is favorable to you in the longer term. Scientists have concluded that its byproduct, AMP, triggers mitochondrial growth.

Intensity Is Not the Effort, but the Output

Back when Deep Purple was recording *Speed King*, preeminent Soviet scientist Prof. Felix Meerson discovered that products of ATP breakdown induce synthesis of mitochondrial proteins. Unfortunately, his discovery was overlooked and had to be made again almost half a century later.

Today we know that something called *AMPK* is the master switch that initiates the chain of events leading to mitochondrial biogenesis. AMPK is a low cellular energy sensor that, as you have guessed from its name, measures the AMP concentration.

To get to maximally achievable AMP numbers and wake up *AMPK*, one must redline the rate of ATP use. The exercise is so intense and its tempo so high that the energy systems are unable to keep up with the ATP expenditure.

ATP deficit starts accumulating after about five seconds of all-out exercise, as soon as the CP system's output starts flagging. Of course, to maximize the amount of AMP, we need to keep at it longer than five seconds.

But not too long, as the intensity will drop…with dire consequences.

"Intensity" has nothing to do with drama—as in the gym motivation slogans aimed at teens yet strangely appearing on 40-year-old dudes' T-shirts. "AMRAP or die!" "For Sparta!"

Intensity is not the effort; it is the output—power output, measured in watts or speed, measured in units of your choice. These external markers reflect the internal rate of ATP use.

A mighty effort is a must, but it is not enough. Even if you somehow sustain a superhuman "nerve force" later in the set, your commands will arrive at your muscles muffled by acid. In addition, the acid will gum up the works that split up ATP (enzyme *ATPase*). As a result, you will not be able to burn through ATP fast enough to produce a lot of AMP.

It is telling that once the intensity of ATP use drops low enough for glycolysis and the aerobic system to replenish it, the ATP deficit is quickly repaid. Soviets discovered that intermediate to elite sprinters and runners experience ATP balance disruption at distances in which the CP mechanism is a major player, up to 400 meters, but not at longer ones. In other words, once your CP system has flamed out, you are suffering for nothing.

"Daddy, what is that red ribbon on the runner's shoulder?"

"It is not a ribbon, daughter, it is his tongue."

From the athlete's point of view, sucking wind at 800 meters qualifies as an emergency much more than sprinting 200 meters. But muscles have a logic of their own. I am sure the cat would agree: When finishing her dinner preparation, it is nice to have a little boost from the emergency system at around 15 seconds. Why would a good hunter be concerned about what happens two minutes later?

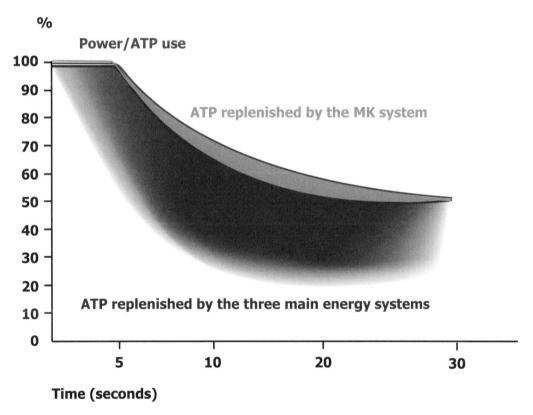

Approximate timeline of ATP demand and supply in brief, all-out dynamic exercise

In summary, to produce AMP, we need to burn through ATP faster than it can be replenished. Research suggests that in all-out dynamic exercise, most AMP is manufactured in the five- to 30-second window, between the time the CP system's output (and thus the total power output) dips and the time the CP is fully exhausted. This seems like a reasonable window for a bout of high-intensity exercise aimed at beefing up the mitochondria.

So far.

...AND THEN THE WHEELS COME OFF

Indeed, in the lab, a single all-out 30-second velo sprint increases the AMP/ATP ratio by as much as 21-fold and significant AMPK increases—signs of upcoming mitochondrial growth—are detected afterward.

In the field, coaches know that 30-second bouts of all-out exercise deliver. Some of the most successful training protocols I taught in the early years of my first kettlebell instructor certification were based on around 20 reps in the snatch and double jerk sprints with 32kg kettlebells. Today, I am convinced that many of the benefits of a 30-second effort are derived during the first 10–20 seconds. There are reasons to occasionally push to 30–45 seconds, but they are outside the foci of this minimalist program.

If the emergency continues and the MK reaction is allowed to run too long, another reaction, *deamination*, kicks in. It demolishes the "A-frames" in some AMP molecules, leaving the phosphates with nothing to attach to.

This is bad news.

First, this reduces the AMP concentration—the signal to the genetic machinery to bulk up the mitochondria. Recall that the target metabolic state is a high AMP-to-ATP ratio. And now we are taking some of the hard-won AMP off the table altogether.

Second, ammonia is a byproduct of this reaction and it is toxic to our cells. Former Master SFG Geoff Neupert even suggested that ammonia toxicity could be one of the factors slowing down fat loss on HIIT.

Third, rebuilding the "A-frames" is a costly and time-consuming process. And while it is taking place, you feel tired and run down, with ATP short of a full stack. Some fish can use up their muscles' ATP and break off the "A-frames" when running from a predator. Then they have to lie helpless under a rock for many hours to restore ATP. Fortunately, humans are not as desperate and we cannot drain our ATP to the point of total immobility. But we still can exhaust it enough to feel dead the day after HIIT. Patients suffering from chronic fatigue syndrome have reduced ATP pools. If you choose to feel that way, metcons are right for you.

Drum roll...a high concentration of lactic acid is the primary driver of deamination.

This is not surprising, considering that one of the goals of this reaction is a desperate attempt to buffer some of the acid.

In all-out exercise, muscle lactate barely budges above its resting level for the first five seconds, while max power is maintained. Then the acid concentration doubles between five and 10 seconds. Then it doubles again from 10 seconds to 20, from 20 seconds to 30, and from 30 seconds to 60.

The amount of acid produced up to 20 seconds is still manageable, but the next doubling is over the top: Even a single 30-second sprint spikes the ammonia levels almost five-fold. Why trash your body for no good reason?

Untrained people deaminate easier than trained athletes, which highlights the irresponsibility of throwing newbies into HIIT. In addition, overtraining lowers one's resistance to deamination. Piling more HIIT workouts on top of each other only makes matters worse.

In disgust, Prof. Yakovlev commented on the "perversion of the muscular activity's chemical nature" taking place during overtraining. He added that the resulting disruption of the aerobic metabolism and a drop in metabolic efficiency lead to significant weight loss in advanced overtraining. Is this why the gen pop loves metcons?

SWEET SPOT IN TIME

What follows is a brief summary of the metabolic events relevant to Q&D. The times are aproximate, as there is a lot of variation among individuals, loads, and exercises.

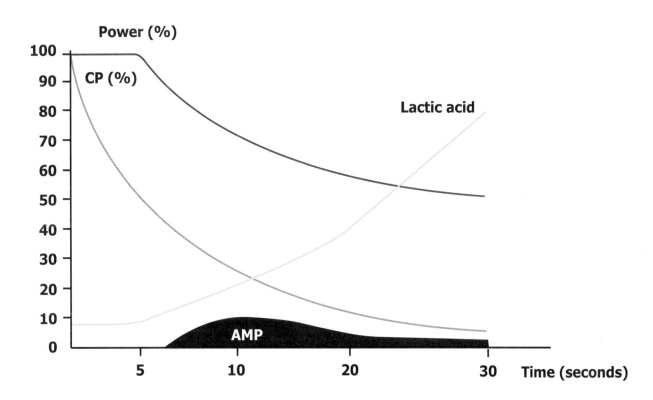

Approximate timeline of the metabolic events most relevant to mitochondrial biogenesis in fast twitch fibers in brief, all-out dynamic exercise: power (P)—synonymous with the rate of ATP turnover, CP concentration, lactic acid concentration, AMP concentration

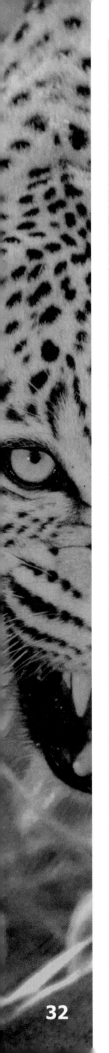

Under Five Seconds

Max power is sustained, as the CP system with its pedal to the metal is keeping up with the replacement of the used-up ATP.

Acid concentration stays around resting levels.

Five to Ten Seconds

Power dips slightly. With the creatine phosphate half depleted, the governor built into the muscles starts throttling down the burn of the remaining CP.

ATP deficit starts accumulating. The "emergency system," myokinase, comes to the rescue and starts disassembling ADP to make ATP and AMP.

Glycolysis rears its ugly reptilian head.

Ten Seconds

CP is depleted by about two-thirds. This is its *critical capacity*, below which it can no longer burn hot.

Glycolysis keeps spreading its leathery wings. It has not resynthesized much ATP yet, but it has already managed to double the acid concentration.

Power noticeably drops, as the used-up ATP is not being fully replenished. The situation becomes desperate and the "emergency system" goes nuclear.

Ten to Twenty Seconds

AMP rapidly accumulates.

Between 10 and 20 seconds, the acid concentration doubles again, reaching its highest acceptable levels.

It is in this 10- to 20-second window that magic takes place, between the instant power noticeably declines and the time glycolysis gains its full steam and starts really gumming up the works with acid.

You are giving your finest effort to sustain max output while your heavyweight energy pathway is fading, but before the acid levels become high enough to ruin everything. The "fourth musketeer" steps into the breach and takes apart ADP to make more ATP, with AMP as a desirable byproduct.

Timing is everything.

Twenty Seconds

The CP system keeps fading. Glycolysis finally gains its feeble full power. It is unable to fill CP's big shoes, being one-and-a-half to two times weaker.

Twenty to Thirty Seconds

Between 20 and 30 seconds, the lactate levels double once more. Desperate to buffer the acid, the body resorts to the highly unfavorable deamination reaction. Some of the hard-won AMP is wiped out.

Thirty Seconds

It is all downhill.

As the power output is halved, ATP use tanks with it. The glycolytic and aerobic systems are now able to keep up with its replenishment; with the ATP supply and demand equivalized, AMP is no longer produced.

Acid keeps climbing, to double again between 30 seconds and 60 seconds. Toxic ammonia and free radicals are accumulating.

The bottom line, based on today's research, is that for most athletes, 15 seconds, plus or minus five seconds, hit the sweet spot, at least for lower body exercises. It takes just as long to stimulate our mitochondria as it took the power cat to catch her dinner.

Within that range, women should stay closer to 20 seconds as they tend to produce less acid and less ammonia than men. This is the same for the less-powerful athletes of both sexes.

Fast-twitch athletes should lean toward 10 seconds, and the fastest drop all the way down to seven or eight seconds.

The more explosive the athlete, the more condensed in time are the described metabolic events within the muscles. ATP and CP burn hotter and deplete faster, the "emergency reaction" comes to the rescue sooner and runs with a greater intensity; deamination also goes live earlier.

German scientists measured the ammonia concentration in up-and-coming young sprinters and middle-distance runners after various distances. After about a 10-second sprint, the former produced noticeable amounts and the latter much less. Thus, it appears that a very powerful athlete will maximize AMP accumulation after just seven or eight seconds. This time window gives the "emergency reaction" two or three seconds to do its job after the power starts fading at about the five-second mark.

FAST 10s—AN EXPLOSIVE EQUAL OF HEAVY FIVES

Working with reps instead of seconds eliminates the headache of customizing the load for individual athletes and for different muscle groups for a given athlete—the upper body tends to be faster twitch than the lower body. The more explosive the athlete, the sooner he or she will complete a given number of reps and vice versa.

In our experiments, we have arrived at the "magic number" of reps that works for most.

That number is 10.

In addition to upping mitochondria's quantity, fast 10s upgrade their quality as well through mechanisms similar to those in classic Soviet anti-glycolytic training. I will explain the nuts and bolts some other time.

Muscle hypertrophy is a collateral benefit of explosive sets of 10. Although there is supposed to be a conflict between myofibrillar and mitochondrial growth, fast 10s deliver both.

Fabio Zonin, Master SFG and the author teaching a Strong Endurance™ seminar

The topic of the muscle growth mechanisms is too broad and interesting to breach here; it deserves a book dedicated to it alone. Today it will suffice to say that, while the exact works remain a mystery, one combination that opens the safe is known:

- ✓ A high rate of ATP use and CP depletion
- ✓ A high magnitude of CP depletion
- ✓ Some acidosis

To be clear, the rate describes how quickly the tank empties; the magnitude how close to "empty" it gets.

Analyze any proven myofibrillar hypertrophy protocol and you will see that, while it may be biased toward one of the above conditions, it checks off all three boxes.

For example, this is how it plays out with heavy reps or grinds.

Singles and doubles build strength faster than any other rep counts, but these gains are unstable and not supported by muscle growth.

Tens rule for pure hypertrophy. Unfortunately, the muscles built with them are not as strong as they look. In addition, 10s make athletes very sore, interfering with other types of training.

While heavy fives do not build mass as quickly as bodybuilding 10s, the quality of this meat is much higher. We are talking about the finest steak versus a mystery meat.

On the strength side, although fives do not build strength as quickly as ultra-low reps, they keep building it year after year, while the progress from singles and doubles fizzles out in weeks.

And soreness, while present, is nowhere close to that resulting from higher reps.

The same dynamics play out with explosive lifts—with double the repetitions. When reps are quick, it takes more of them to reach the same metabolic conditions. For instance, for fast fiber hypertrophy, sets of fast 20s cannot be beat: The rate of CP depletion is high during the first half of the set; by the end, the magnitude of CP depletion is maximal and acidosis is high.

But there is a price to pay. Westside Barbell's mastermind Louie Simmons, an early adopter of hard style kettlebell training for powerlifting assistance, found out that fast 20s made him too sore and tired, so he chose to stick with fast 10s. Listen to Louie.

10x10, Reloaded

For the fast 10s to work as promised, you must take enough rest between them.

Brett Jones, StrongFirst's Director of Education, has observed that almost universally, gireviks rest less than they ought to. They may not realize that both CP and pH must recover, the former to fuel another intense bout and the latter to avoid a whole lot of the problems discussed earlier.

CP recovers rapidly, but pH takes forever. It takes our bodies about 30 minutes to clear all the lactic acid produced by a single 100-meter sprint! Full recovery is obviously out of the question; a reasonable compromise must be found. And Prof. Nikolay Volkov found it for us when studying circa 15-second sprints for other reasons: It is two-and-a-half to three minutes.

Thus, programming becomes very straightforward: a set of 10 every three minutes.

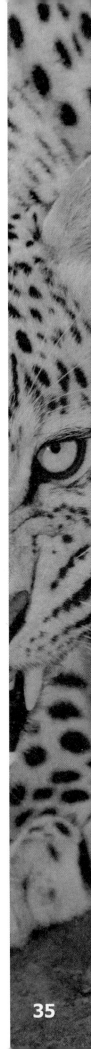

And do not dare to take less rest, no matter how highly you think of your conditioning! If the super athlete I am about to introduce takes the full three minutes, so should you.

The US military special operator I will call "Victor" is an extraordinary athlete. On the wrong side of 40, he is a good decade past the expiration date in this line of duty where, even if one does not get shot, he gets worn down. Victor not only remains healthy against all odds, but bests young guns in feats like multiple one-arm chins and 100-mile ultra races. He wrote to me:

> Your Strong Endurance research has validated many of the training methods I have been using intuitively for the past 15 years, and you have provided a great framework for me to continue to program healthy progress…

> Back in 2009, I added 12- to 15-second sprints in the form of stadium stair sprints, and I did them on a 3:00 interval. I usually did 10 explosive pushups at the top of the stairs. This is very similar to what you described in Strong Endurance. Even back then, I felt intuitively that these short, intense intervals were much easier on the body than traditional 400- to 800-meter intervals. I continue to use this type of training today.

I will interrupt Victor to express my admiration for the rare blend of intuition and intelligence that enabled him to arrive at these load parameters. It took me four years of dusty biochem texts to get here.

> Another great side effect of this type of training is that I never experienced any major training injuries or the exercise burnout many of my peers experienced in the Special Operations community. Many of my peers in SOF are very fit and are able to perform; however, they suffer from high cortisol, low testosterone, and many have sleep problems. When you add the sleep and emotional stressors on a deployment, many of these guys are setting themselves up for serious long-term health problems.

> I would love to see more of this type of education and training in SOF. Most guys I worked with do a good job of training for performance, but at the expense of their long-term health. I believe this approach is very shortsighted. Alactic training would allow them to maintain their performance goals in a way that does not compromise long-term health and function.

Three minutes is a perfect compromise between effectiveness and efficiency, the point of diminishing returns. Within that time frame, CP is rapidly refueled; after that mark, it gets replenished drip by drip.

How many sets of 10?

10.

No, it is not just another nice round number. Prof. Volkov's research also teaches us that a maximum of 10 sets of circa 15-second all-out repeats may be done with the above rest periods if we insist on negligible power decline and minimal glycolytic involvement. Go beyond, and you will be training something else as your CP stores progressively shrink while your pH keeps falling. So, do not go there.

Ten sets also neatly meet the compromise between the metabolic demands optimal for building mitochondria and myofibrils—enough for the latter and not too many for the former.

One hundred reps was a maximal training volume per exercise per training session in the Soviet weightlifting methodology, especially when hypertrophy was emphasized. Prof. Arkady Vorobyev explains:

> Under the influence of a load on the muscles, depending on its type, the function of structural elements of the tissue (an anabolic reaction) or energetic economization of structures responsible for expenditure and synthesis of energy and muscular work (endurance training), may be strengthened...It goes without saying that such specialization of structural elements depending on the type of activity is quite relative. Muscle work leads to a simultaneous expenditure of energetic and plastic resources. But the type of activity determines the direction of expenditure and the following restoration of the biological system.

Evidently, this is why weightlifters who double or triple the optimal volume do not experience much strength gain. They "were more enduring but less strong compared to athletes training with lower load volumes, as they primarily activated the processes of energy production rather than protein synthesis," concludes Vorobyev.

10x10 it is.

Yes, it does look suspiciously similar to *Kettlebell Simple & Sinister*—except you are not to compress the rest periods: one set every three minutes, no matter what, even if you feel totally recovered. Your feelings do not matter.

THE MELODY IS IN THE RESTS

Straight 10x10 deliver. But they can be improved upon.

Something remarkable happens when you keep the sets, reps, and total session duration constant—10x10 within 30 minutes—but stagger the sets in a particular manner.

"There's no music in a 'rest'...but there's the making of music in it," wrote John Ruskin, an artist, writer, and art critic from Victorian England. "And people are always missing that part of the life-melody...People are always talking of perseverance, and courage, and fortitude; but patience is the finest and worthiest part of fortitude—and the rarest too...For patience lies at the root of all pleasures, as well as of all powers."

More biochemistry coming right up. Enjoy the pain.

Earlier, out of mercy, I presented a simplified picture of the metabolic conditions needed to pull the AMPK trigger and turn on the mitochondria building machinery: accumulate a lot of AMP.

While scientists are in agreement on that point, some have concluded that there is more to the story. Accumulation of *free creatine*, the product of CP breakdown, may be even more important.

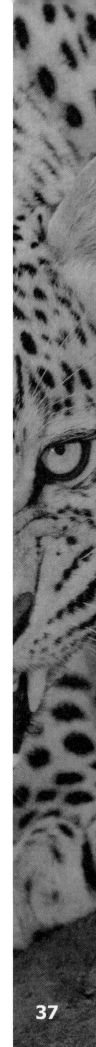

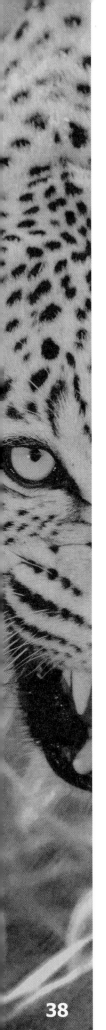

And it may be the rate rather than the magnitude of fuel depletion that increases AMPK activity. Most likely, both the rate and the magnitude have an effect. And that presents a conflict.

Our bodies have all sorts of built-in governors designed to prevent us from running ourselves dead. As you recall, the enzyme that breaks down the "rocket fuel" of creatine phosphate (*creatine kinase*) has such a governor built in. The more CP is exhausted, the more its throttle is closed.

"I want it all and I want it now."

Since the first sub-goal is duration driven and the second is intensity driven, a compromise is unavoidable. This brings us back to our approximately 15 seconds, where neither the rate nor the magnitude of fuel depletion is maximal but both are substantial.

So far nothing has changed in our program design if we stick with the *repeat method*, as in the above 10x10. However, it changes if we employ the *interval-serial method*, a powerful weapon in elite athletes' arsenal.

Prof. Leonid Matveev classified rest intervals between exercise bouts as *stress, ordinary,* and *stimulation*.

The stimulation interval is the stuff of "greasing the groove" and is not relevant to this book.

Stress intervals are short enough to progressively accumulate fatigue. This is interval training as you know it.

Ordinary intervals are in between—they allow more or less full recovery but no more. This is the repeat method used in the Q&D 10x10 protocol.

The interval-serial method combines stress and ordinary rest periods. It features multiple series, or groups of several sets. Within each series, sets are done with incomplete rest between them, aiming for a cumulative fuel depletion toward the end of a series. Then a longer rest is taken between series.

Why bother?

Because recovery is not one thing. Multiple functions must recuperate, and each does so at its own pace. As you recall, CP is fast to bounce back and pH is slow.

To a coach, the interval-serial method offers an opportunity to customize the metabolic events in a way that is impossible to achieve with straight intervals or repeats. We can push chosen types of fatigue while restraining others, like a sound engineer at a mixing board boosting select frequencies while cutting others.

I wanted to achieve a rapid *and* deep depletion of cellular fuels—and suspected that the interval-serial method would be the answer.

A Rugby Lesson

The method did not fail. And the reason lay in training the quality that game coaches call the *repeat sprint ability* (RSA).

RSA is the ability to perform multiple short sprints (typically less than 10 seconds) with little rest between them (less than 60 seconds) with a minimal performance decline. Metabolically, it is totally different from pop HIIT favorites like 400-meter intervals or "Tabatas."

Repeat sprint ability studies—especially by Russian Prof. Nikolay Volkov, Australian Dr. Paul Dawson, and Swede Dr. Paul Balsom—were very helpful in identifying the loads that produce the target metabolic state for building mitochondria in fast fibers. RSA researchers did not set out to discover the training load that triggers mitochondrial biogenesis. They were after the parameters that enabled game athletes to sustain near-max sprinting prowess over and over. Fortunately, their goal was closely aligned with mine.

RSA researchers consistently kept arriving at 30 seconds of total sprint time within a series. Performance stayed at a high level up to that point—e.g., only an eight- to 10-percent peak power decrease after five six-second velo sprints done every 30 seconds. However, as soon as the half-a-minute threshold was breached, the speed and the power rapidly tanked and acid quickly accumulated.

The above eight- to 10-percent power drop-off is awesomely small compared with a 40- to 50-percent decline after a single 30-second velo sprint. And since there is a linear relationship between the exercise intensity (power) and the rate of CP depletion, this means we are able to run the CP system hot for a full 30 seconds in a series, not just the first 10 seconds of a 30-second bout.

However, a single 30-second sprint is superior in one aspect. It achieves a near-total CP exhaustion—a series of several bursts totaling 30 seconds still reaches an impressive nearly three-quarter CP depletion.

And an awesome one-third of ATP depletion.

This is far more impressive than it sounds. Your body is very protective of its ATP. No matter how hard you push, you cannot deplete it by more than 20–40 percent.

On our balance sheet, we have depleted ATP and CP as rapidly as possible, depleted ATP as deeply as possible, and CP significantly. Mission accomplished.

Once I was convinced the numbers added up to fit the mitochondrial biogenesis in the fast fibers model, I had another break. I came across an Iranian-American-Estonian study—does that sound like something out of a Tom Clancy novel?—that literally applied the RSA load parameters identified by the authors mentioned earlier to the training of advanced Iranian wrestlers, without speculating about the underlying cellular mechanisms:

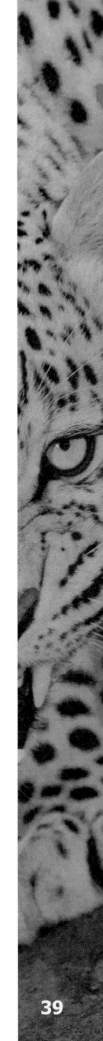

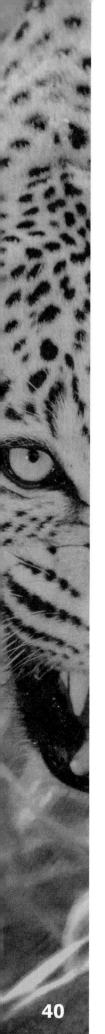

- Thirty-five-meter sprints (about five seconds)

- Six sprints per series

- Ten-second rest between sprints

- Three minutes of rest between series

- Three to six series per session

- Two times a week

In just four weeks, these top athletes made great improvements on many fronts. Their time to exhaustion at a given speed increased by almost a third. Their peak and mean power on the 30-second veloergometer test significantly improved. Even their VO_2 max went up by more than five percent, which is a lot for the conditioning machines that wrestlers are, especially from a protocol that is not overly demanding on the "cardio."

The athletes' testosterone and the testosterone-to-cortisol ratio increased significantly, while cortisol tended to decrease. This is great news not just for muscle building, but more importantly, for health.

I applied this protocol literally to two-arm overspeed eccentric kettlebell swings and tested it with the help of the StrongFirst team. All subjects, ranging from a nine-year-old girl to experienced fighters, had great results.

THE FINISHING TOUCHES

I continued analyzing the metabolic events and experimenting with different set lengths.

When the chosen exercise is a sprint, its duration has to be limited to less than six seconds, the acceleration phase. Once the athlete has reached the top speed, no matter how high it is, power leaves the building. Without acceleration—a change in velocity—there is no force and thus, no power.

Sprinters typically take about six seconds or 50–60 meters to accelerate to top speed from a static start. Game athletes need 30–45 meters and non-athletes even less than that. This means the 40-yard dash from American football fully qualifies as a power event, but only a fraction of a 100-meter sprint does.

This under-six-second time limit does not apply to non-locomotion exercises like swings and pushups: there is a new acceleration in every rep. We experimented with different set and rep combinations totaling 20 reps, about 30 seconds of swings. The most effective and user-friendly options turned out to be 5/4 and 10/2, where the first number is reps and the second represents the sets:

5/4

- Five reps per set
- One set every 30 seconds
- Four sets per series

10/2

- Ten reps per set
- One set every 60 seconds
- Two sets per series

We tinkered with different rests between sets within a series and chose the classic guideline for alactic interval training by Profs. Edward Fox and Donald Matthews: a 1:3 work-to-rest ratio. Recall that within a series, we are doing intervals rather than repeats; hence, the recovery is supposed to be incomplete.

We stayed with five series of 20, a total of 100 reps based on the Russian training guidelines advising to limit the CP system training volume to less than two-and-a-half minutes per session.

A Strong Endurance™ seminar in Italy

From the RSA research, we knew the rest between series of RSA sprints must be no less than three minutes—and preferably four minutes and even longer.

The 5/4 protocol is aimed at maximizing the rate of fuel burn and the 10/2 at a deeper depletion. Higher acidity in the latter is also supposed to deliver a hypertrophy WTHE.

We tested extensively. Both versions yielded excellent performance results, similar for both set and rep schemes. As predicted, 10/2 quickly built muscle, while 5/4 did not. There were also reports of gentlemen rapidly bulking up 10 pounds on 10/2 and losing all this new mass after switching to 5/4—without any loss of power or endurance.

These are peak power readings for an experienced girevik doing the Q&D protocol with 10/2 x 5 of two-arm 40kg swings and pushups. Note that the swing peak power does not deteriorate toward the end. In fact, it tends to go up slightly, presumably because of the lack of a warm-up. In the pushup, power dips, but within an acceptable range. The subject commented that the pushup power would have undoubtedly taken a steep dive had he done one more series.

Gains in power were expected and so were improvements in sport-specific endurance in games and combat sports. But some WTHEs were totally out of the blue.

Matthew Flaherty, SFG/SFB/SFL, did a 100-plus-mile mountain bike ride in Colorado. Later, with no changes in his training other than an addition of six weeks of 033 swings twice a week, he did another ride, the Tour de Steamboat:

Two mountain bike rides separated by Q&D			
	Bike ride #1	Bike ride #2:	Improvement
Distance	108 miles	116 miles	+8 miles
Climb	6890'	7110'	+220'
Average climb	6–7% grade 3 mph	7% grade 7.5 mph	+50% faster at about the same grade
Riding time	14 hours	9:52:10	Over 4 hours

As you can see, the second ride was longer and steeper, yet the rider completed it four hours earlier!

Sean Sewell, a Colorado mountain man who was introduced to Strong Endurance™ protocols by Eric Frohardt, SFG, writes:

There were several programs in the Strong Endurance manual, but the two that jumped out at me were 033C and 044[3]. They are beautiful in their simplicity and relatively easy to do. At first, I was not used to the added rest time required in these programs, but before long I understood its benefit.

After a week, I could already feel the difference in my practices in the gym. My resting heart rate went down for the first time in years. My strength went up quickly. I was not tired after practice and I had more energy. At the end of the 033C and 044 protocols, the data was pretty conclusive. Resting HR went from 72 to 56; HRV went from 60s to 80s (sometimes even 90s), and strength improved quickly. I went from using 20kg to 32kg.

But surely these quick and intense practices could not positively affect hours of hiking at 12,000-plus feet. Time to put it to the test. I went to one of my favorite backcountry ski spots for a four-hour hike with a friend.

After reaching a high alpine lake, we stopped to have a snack. It was then I realized how well the Strong Endurance protocols were working. I looked at my hiking partner, who is in good shape, and he was winded, as anyone should be after a good hike. I was not fazed, though. The training works.

---

[3] The StrongFirst Experimental Protocol 044 is the snatch version of Q&D.

PART III: THE POWER DRILLS

THE POWER DRILLS OF CHOICE

Many popular minimalist training programs are made up of three lifts. A three-legged stool is most stable and all that jazz. But why would you want a stool if you could have a Harley? Two wheels are more than enough when you are going fast.

Years ago I came to the conclusion that an ultra-minimalist program must have only two lifts: a push and a pull, or, rather, a hip hinge.

The deadlift plus the side press in *Power to the People!*

The snatch plus the bent press in *The Russian Kettlebell Challenge*

The snatch plus the military press in *Enter the Kettlebell!*

The swing plus the get-up in *Enter the Kettlebell!* and *Kettlebell Simple & Sinister*

The ***** plus the ****** in *The Quick and the Dead*

Steve Freides, Senior SFG, made a post on the StrongFirst forum entitled *Two-Lift Programs*:

Balance is overrated. The idea that a lifting program must touch on all the "basic human movements" is fundamentally flawed. One should move in as many varied ways as possible, at least from time to time, but that doesn't mean heavily loading every possible movement pattern. A lifting program can do what a lifting program needs to do and only contain two lifts. A lifting program doesn't need to be balanced—a life does.

Steve keeps his training minimalist—and gets his balance by competing in all-around lifts[4]. Freides holds over 20 masters' records, world and American, in exotica such as the "Steinborn lift" and the "Inman mile." The former is a powerlifting squat, except that it starts and ends with the bar on the platform. The lifter has to maneuver the barbell onto the shoulders with complicated body language, squat below parallel, and then respectfully return the bar to the platform in the same controlled manner as lifted. The latter is death march with 150 percent of the athlete's bodyweight on a yoke sitting on the shoulders.

Dr. Mike Prevost agreed:

This approach can be really effective…include some Hindu pushups, bodyweight squats, yoga poses, a bit of sprinting, some flexibility work, balance work (like on a slack line), lots of walking, some practice with break falls and rolls, swimming...

Besides, given the carryover from select kettlebell exercises to many seemingly unrelated events, is your minimalist program really unbalanced?

---

[4] For specifics, go to all-around lifting federations' sites usawa.com/about-us and iawa.uk/about.

Here is how I arrived at the winning one-two combination for *The Quick and the Dead*.

For the sake of efficiency, the Q&D exercises need to **involve many muscle groups** and have an impressive record of **wide carryover and many WTHEs**.

Our drills of choice must **enable maximal expression of power**, which means a **long range of motion** (ROM) to give plenty of distance for acceleration.

This is why the kettlebell clean is not a Q&D choice: Its ROM is short. It is a better move for strength than power.

Also, unlike pure power training in which a leisurely cadence and relaxing between reps are encouraged, the WTHE-bearing Q&D drills must enable a quick tempo. High RPM are imposed by the requirement to drain ATP and CP as quickly as possible.

Understand that max power and high cadence are in conflict with each other—like the length and the frequency of a sprinter's strides.

A boxer throwing a rapid-fire combination of punches cannot put nearly as much oomph into any one of them as into a single-focused widow maker.

A far less impressive example of high cadence draining the power are "Nazi" kettlebell snatches, where a lockout is never reached all in the name of a higher tempo.

According to our understanding of the prerequisite metabolic events, power must be prioritized over cadence. In other words, use the **highest cadence possible without compromising the power or cutting the ROM**.

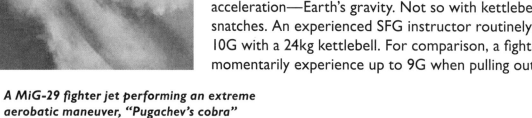

This makes kettlebell swings and snatches uniquely qualified because they enable *overspeed eccentrics*.

Dr. Mel Siff explained this high-concept technique:

> *Instead of lowering the [weight] slowly or allowing it to drop under gravitational acceleration, deliberately pull the [weight] downward as fast as you can, stop the downward motion...as rapidly as you can...to accelerate the [weight] upward into a powerful concentric movement.*

With most explosive exercises, even very fine ones like depth jumps and jerks, you are limited to 1G of downward acceleration—Earth's gravity. Not so with kettlebell swings and snatches. An experienced SFG instructor routinely pulls over 10G with a 24kg kettlebell. For comparison, a fighter jet pilot may momentarily experience up to 9G when pulling out of a dive.

A MiG-29 fighter jet performing an extreme aerobatic maneuver, "Pugachev's cobra"

Overspeed eccentric swings and snatches—not content with the 1G of gravity on the way down, a seasoned hard style girevik accelerates the kettlebell up to 10G with an aggressive swimming-like arm action.

The benefits of overspeed eccentrics are awesome and many: jumping prowess, touch-and-go reactive ability, resilience, strength, even hypertrophy. Most of these have been written about; one has not.

Overspeed eccentric swings and snatches with light to moderate weights are perfect for inducing the metabolic events that spark mitochondrial biogenesis in fast fibers. They enable both max power and a very high tempo—a unique and contradictory combination, like a rapid-fire series of knockout punches.

A power drill of choice must **continually load the same muscle groups**.

For example, in the kettlebell swing, the posterior chain is constantly working. The hammies may be more engaged on the bottom and the glutes on the top, but neither muscle group gets much rest.

In contrast, in the snatch, the upper back and the triceps take over once the 'bell is halfway up, giving the lower body a break.

Nevertheless, the snatch more than makes up for this shortcoming with a tremendous power output over a very long trajectory—twice that of a swing. The rests the lower and upper body receive will be very brief indeed.

This is not so with the clean-and-jerk. Although it involves more muscle groups than any lift I can think of, the long cycle relays the work between muscle groups in such a way that no participant gets too smoked: dip, drive, second dip, lock out, dip, and catch. The C&J's multistage nature slows down the cellular fuels' depletion. It is a tremendous asset in some types of training (such as classic Soviet anti-glycolytic protocols), but it works against you when you are trying to use up your substrates ASAP.

In contrast, the one-arm "Viking" push press (VPP) meets the prerequisites, although not chosen for Q&D because it is unsuitable to many ladies. What makes the VPP superior to other kettlebell pushes is its ability to maintain a high cadence.

To perform a VPP, push press the first rep as usual, then drop the kettlebell to your chest, dip your knees to absorb the impact—and immediately shoot the 'bell up again without resetting for the next rep.

The double VPP, on the other hand, is not optimized for Q&D: The weights that are right for the quads are too light for the triceps.

In the classic push press, the additional knee dip slows the tempo.

The strict military press does not work either, as the 'bell starts flailing when the cadence picks up.

These are all great exercises, just not for Q&D.

The floor pushup is the Q&D push of choice—classic and democratic.

Parallel bar dips also worked great for the subjects whose shoulders could take this controversial movement, but since Q&D was conceived as an egalitarian "power to the people!" type program, dips did not make the final cut..

The drills of choice must have a **ballistic component** for the sake of anti-fragility and carryover to athletic events, professional demands, and life's challenges. In other words, veloergometer sprints might build your mitochondria, but you will not net the collateral benefits.

The parallel bar dip is my push of choice for Q&D.

On the other hand, too much ballistic loading could spell trouble orthopedically, at least with a heavy weight such as one's bodyweight. The Q&D drills of choice are those you **can do safely for hundreds of reps a week**, every week. That excludes depth jumps and, for many, all jumps. You are looking at about 10,000 reps per year and your knees and feet will not thank you.

In summary, the Q&D exercises must meet the following exacting requirements:

- ✓ Recruit many muscle groups
- ✓ Have a wide carryover
- ✓ Produce many WTHEs
- ✓ Have a long range of motion and allow a maximal expression of power
- ✓ Enable a high cadence without compromising the power or cutting the ROM
- ✓ Continually load the same muscle groups
- ✓ Have a ballistic component
- ✓ Can be done safely for hundreds of reps a week, every week

And the winners are…swings and pushups.

Ilaria Scopece, SFG/SFB:

"The hard style swing is very important for the athlete who practices a combat sport. In boxing, the impulse starts from the ground and rises along the leg; the hips rotate thanks to the glutes, the impulse propagates through the core to the upper limbs and finally moves through the upper limb that is about to strike. The swing allows you to explosively train the hip snap and the core, and the kettlebell float relates to the technique of the boxing jab."

"The pushups in this plan are performed explosively. This movement is similar to the impact of a punch in its starting acceleration and final contraction and tension."

The snatch is a special case. More about it later.

Swings: two-arm or one-arm?

Yes. Both have their advantages. The former enable greater power and a higher cadence, while the latter train the grip, lats, glute medius, and other players that chill on the bench in bilateral exercise. Q&D employs both.

Dr. Craig Marker, Senior SFG, a 185-pounder with a 485-pound raw deadlift, did over three months of 033 using two-arm swings for sets of 10 exclusively. He swung 40kg, the weight that enabled max power production.

In spite of barely snatching in training, he put up PR 100 reps in five minutes with 32kg at the Tactical Strength Challenge[5] (TSC), an impressive performance when one specifically trains for it—and exceptional when one does not. Q&D is not cardio intensive and 40kg two-arm swings do not challenge the grip nearly as much as one-arm snatches with 32kg.

Craig matched his PR in the deadlift, in spite of pulling exactly two DL reps in the previous six months, both super light, done to demonstrate technique to a student.

He also put up excellent 19 tactical pullups—very strict and neck to the bar—with an extra 22 pounds, without doing pullups in training.

The Q&D protocol with two-arm kettlebell swings enabled Dr. Marker to do 19 tactical pullups—very strict and neck to the bar—with an extra 22 pounds, without doing pullups in training. He is demonstrating the correct finish of a tactical pullup wearing a weighted vest from 5.11 Tactical®.

Dr. Marker experienced other WTHEs. His free testosterone went up 110 units after six weeks of Q&D, which was not surprising. But then Craig somehow rewound his body clock. Based on telomere testing, before the 033 protocol, he was eight years younger than the number on his driver's license. After six months of Q&D training and no other changes in his lifestyle, he was 14 years younger.

---

[5]To learn more about the Tactical Strength Challenge go to strongfirst.com/achieve/tactical-strength-challenge/.

With all that in mind, swings and power pushups are our minimalist drills of choice, a classic one-two combination.

The snatch is an alternative Q&D selection for the ultra-minimalist. Both pulls and pushes are covered.

Why not make the snatch "the" Q&D choice? Because the shoulders of some hard-living types cannot meet the exacting mobility and stability demanded by this elitist exercise.

But if you check off all the boxes, there are some heavy-duty WTHEs to collect.

If you are reading this book, you were sold on the kettlebell snatch a long time ago, so I will not waste your time reciting the laundry list you already know. I will just highlight a couple of especially unusual WTHEs delivered by Q&D snatching: Military press and pullup strength increases.

Over the years, many of our SFG instructors saw military press improvement, or at least maintenance, from a significant volume of heavy snatches, plus impressive upper back and shoulder hypertrophy. But on Q&D (Plan 044) some of our subjects ended up pressing a lot heavier than what they were snatching.

Mike Torres, SFG Team Leader, reports:

I have been doing Plan 044 three days per week consistently, starting with a 28kg and occasionally moving up to the 32kg. Yesterday I felt inspired to press a kettlebell for the first time in a while. For reference, when I got my half-bodyweight press of 36kg, I had trained hard for it for almost nine months—and even then, it only went up on one side. It felt lucky. I haven't pressed heavy or high volume since then.

For some reason, that 36kg looked tiny yesterday—so I dragged it out, for some reason fully expecting to press it. It went up EASILY on the right (no slowdown at all), which was the first time I had done that. And then it went up just as easily on the left. It was as if the 'bell was mocking me for stressing so much about that press for the first half of the year.

The WTH effect from all that snatching was in full effect! It's pretty exciting—since it wasn't what I was expecting from Strong Endurance Plan 044. I've definitely seen some upper body hypertrophy—traps and triceps. Grip feels stronger too.

Shawn Reed did the snatch-only Plan 044 for six weeks:

	Pre-test	Post-test 6 Weeks Later
Snatch reps in 30 seconds, 32kg	15 left, 15 right	18 left, 18 right
Military press, 48kg, RM	0 left, 1 right	2 left, 3 right
Pullup, 1RM	32kg	48kg
Bodyweight	233 pounds	239 pounds

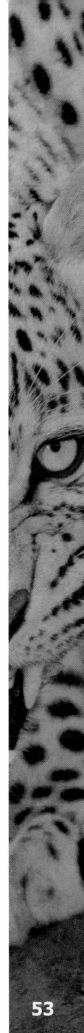

You can see that Shawn packed on a solid pound of meat per week and improved his snatch performance—as expected. But his pullup and military press strength going up were pure WTHEs.

Shawn improved his Beast pressing strength not only without pressing—but even without touching anything remotely heavy for him. He was snatching 32kg, merely two-thirds of his military press IRM.

Results such as these are not unusual among experienced gireviks who already know how to military press. If you think about it, the snatch is a swing followed by a fast press, so this makes some sense.

I am sure you also noticed that Shawn's strict pullup strength jumped from adding 32kg to 48kg. We have seen this snatch WTH effect many times over the years. Derek Toshner, a Senior SFG who has been dominating TSC for years, writes:

> I would like to suggest that lots of snatching is the largest reason we perform well for the TSC. Our pullups actually get worse when we practice them with high repetitions, so we don't practice them that way. I, along with our members, have noted that when we ignore pullups and perform lots of snatches leading up to the TSC, our max number of pullups increases. Snatching also seems to shred body fat, and one of the best ways I've found as a rock climber to increase pullups is to lose excess weight.

Shawn gained weight rather than losing it, so it was something else. Whatever it is, we will take it.

On to the performance standards and the testing protocols for swings plus pushups or snatches.

Derek Toshner, Senior SFG: *"You get on the Plan 044 and start snatching, the next thing you know, you are climbing 5.10s and you have not been rock climbing in months. It's like...there it is! The grip strength, right?"*

THE SWING: VIOLENT AS A HUNT IN THE SAVANNAH

This book is not for beginners and I expect the reader to be more than competent in both swings and power pushups. The following is not to teach you how, but to remind you what the StrongFirst technique standards are.

ONE-ARM KETTLEBELL SWING TECHNIQUE

Task:

Swing a single kettlebell

Condition:

Swing a kettlebell back between your legs and then in front of you up to chest level for 10 repetitions.

Standard:

1. The back is neutral. The neck is slightly extended or neutral at the bottom of the swing.

2. The heels, toes, and the balls of the feet are planted and the knees track the toes.

3. The working shoulder is packed.

4. The kettlebell handle passes above the knees during the backswing.

5. The arm is straight in the bottom position.

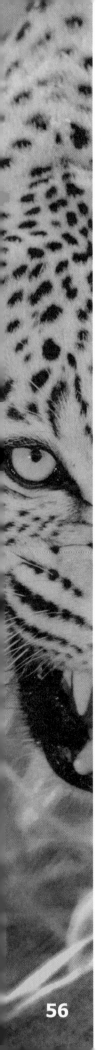

6. There is no forward knee movement (increasing ankle dorsiflexion) on the upswing.

7. The body forms a straight line at the top of the swing. The hips and knees extend fully, the spine is neutral.

8. The kettlebell forms an extension of the straight arm at the top of the swing. A slight elbow bend is acceptable.

9. The biomechanical breathing match (inhale on the way down and forcefully exhale on the way up).

10. The abs and glutes visibly contract at the top of the swing.

11. The kettlebell floats for an instant at the top of the swing.

Change a couple of words to plural and all of the above applies to two-arm swings.

To select the correct weight, choose one of the two following tests. Test after a warm-up of choice. Every rep must comply with the SFG standards. You may use overspeed eccentrics to the extent you are accustomed to doing them with the given weight.

Option One
Kettlebell Swing Accelerometer Test

If you have access to an accelerometer or a force plate, test yourself swinging different size kettlebells. Do not reflexively grab the biggest 'bell. Remember that max power resides in the sweet spot between heavy and light.

Test in sets of five, with five minutes of rest between sets, to identify the kettlebell that enables maximal power expression.

Repeat the test two more times with the same weight and record the highest reading.

Option Two
Kettlebell Swing Long Sprint Test

Find the kettlebell you can "sprint" with for 20–30 seconds.

This is a poor test for measuring power, akin to estimating one's 40-yard dash by testing a 200-meter sprint. But it does the job of selecting the correct resistance.

Make sure not to lose the float or the glute contraction on the top of each rep. Use chalk generously to make sure grip is not the limiting factor.

The clock starts when the kettlebell leaves the ground. It stops at 30 seconds. The time it takes the kettlebell to swing back and then to the ground after the last rep does not count toward the 30-second total—think of it as a sprinter's movement past the finish line.

Count only perfect, explosive reps. Instruct your testing partner to stop the clock and the test earlier than 30 seconds if technique or power are compromised. If the timer is stopped before 30 seconds, record the time it was stopped for comparison with future tests' results.

If you have been unable to swing the given kettlebell explosively for at least 20 seconds, it is too heavy to use in Q&D. Rest and repeat the test with a lighter kettlebell.

If, on the other hand, you have completed 30 seconds with high power and room to spare, rest and repeat the test with a heavier kettlebell. Ten minutes of rest is required between all long sprint tests, regardless of swing type or kettlebell weight.

Retest all drills once every four to six weeks, on a session after a minimal volume day of 40 reps, as described later in the book. Keep your warm-ups consistent, as well as the time of the day you are testing, the rests between sets, the shoes or lack of thereof, etc.

Test your drills in the following order:

1. One-arm swing, the non-dominant arm

2. One-arm swing, the dominant arm

3. Power pushup

4. Two-arm swing

This is a lot of tests and a bit of time, but it is time well spent—you are not just testing; you are training. The above load qualifies as *glycolytic power repeats,* a smart type of glycolytic training that maximizes the benefits of acid while minimizing the problems caused by it. More about this type of training in the future.

You may choose to test the pushup and the two-arm swing on separate days, one or two days after the one-arm swing test.

THE PUSHUP: A CLASSIC, REMASTERED

Behold the StrongFirst pushup standard.

PUSHUP TECHNIQUE

Task:

Pushup

Condition:

From the pushup plank position on your palms or fists, bend your elbows and lower your entire body, then press back up for 10 repetitions.

Standard:

1. The spine is neutral.

2. The entire body forms a straight line—no piking or sagging. The hips and shoulders descend and ascend at the same rate.

3. The abs and the glutes are braced.

4. The feet are no wider than the shoulders.

5. The shoulders stay depressed—anti-shrugged.

6. The shoulder blades retract at the bottom of each rep.

7. The elbows may not flare more than 45 degrees.

8. Descend at least until the tips of the elbows are above the tops of the shoulders.*

9. The chest may gently brush the deck, but not bounce off it.

10. The stomach and the knees may not touch the deck at any time.

11. Press back up until the elbows fully extend.

12. Audibly power breathe on the top of each rep.

*   *If you have long arms and a small rib cage that force you to compromise your shoulder position to achieve this ROM, go as deep as you can while maintaining the correct shoulder alignment.*

You may do your pushups on your palms or fists.

The former enable greater strength and power, as the pressure on the heels of the palms amplifies triceps strength and makes it easier to bring the lats into action. The downside of traditional palm pushups is they may be hard on some athletes' wrists.

The fist pushup, in contrast, not only spares the wrist joints, but also strengthens the surrounding muscles.

Yes, you could use pushup handles, but that would be below your dignity.

Everyone but bare-knuckle fighters should load the lower part of the fist, the little and the ring fingers. This lines up the load with the stronger of the two forearm bones, closer to the indestructible armpit than the vulnerable shoulder.

If you are a martial artist who says "No" to gloves, use the first two knuckles of the index and the middle fingers. As you know, these knuckles are much sturdier than the other two—boxers break their hands in street fights because they punch as if they were protected by gloves. The downside of this load placement is that the force is projected onto the top of the shoulder instead of its sturdy underside. Experienced karatekas mitigate this problem somewhat by "making a fist starting from the little finger" and thus trying to connect the arm to the body through the armpit more than the top of the shoulder.

The above applies to all pushups, and now we move specifically to explosive ones.

Start the first rep from the bottom, lying prone with your hands on the floor (the only time your belly may touch the deck). Brace and explode. Do not cheat with your knees.

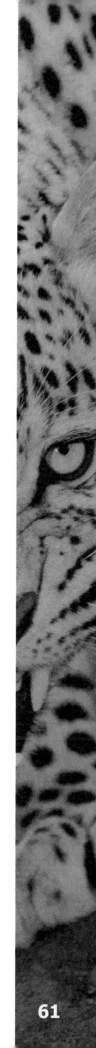

Practice this dead start during the tests and the work sets alike. There are several reasons behind this.

First, it develops starting strength.

Second, it will help you optimize your hand placement. Move around and adjust until you feel your lats against your tris and your palms or fists positioned where there is no joint stress and you feel loaded to explode.

If your build prevents you from safely going this deep, skip dead starts and do your Q&D pushups in the traditional manner starting from the top.

Pushups must be maximally explosive. Aim for a high cadence as well, but make sure to achieve a full lockout each time.

Avoid the temptation to whip your neck in high-tempo pushups. Focusing on lowering and lifting your chest rather than your nose should help. "Packing" your neck might as well.

There are two opposite ways to lock out powerfully.

One, jump—or at least intend to, with the heels of your palms or your fists unloading on the top of each rep.

Two, "root." Visualize attempting to leave deep imprints of your palms or fists in the ground.

Pick one.

Uncommitted reps with the elbows never locking is one of the reasons fighters fail to develop striking power from pushups. Save "soft elbows" for shadow boxing; this is not the time.

Prof. Vladimir Zatsiorsky explains:

> *To develop a quick expression of strength, the dynamic effort method is used…moving some submaximal resistance with maximal speed and a full range of motion. If movements with a limited range (a stop) are used, undesirable coordination may develop…the agonists, barely having started working, immediately turn off and the antagonists breaking the movement become active. If such coordination becomes habitual, then the finish phase would be performed insufficiently actively in other movements as well. This is why it is recommended, for example, to finish a squat with a jump, use throws, strikes, etc.*

Opposite of jumping in its intention, the martial arts technique of *rooting* has the same effect of enabling one to express full power at the lockout without putting on the brakes. StrongFirst teaches rooting to the students of all strength modalities—kettlebell, bodyweight, and barbell.

The above admonition by Zatsiorsky is especially vital when you are aiming for a high cadence. Cutting the reps short is tempting. Do not. In Q&D, power takes priority over cadence. Always.

The negative is a free fall. If you are strong enough to be using a band for extra resistance, you will be getting the added benefit of an overspeed eccentric. With or without a band, bend your elbows, absorb the kinetic energy, and explosively release it into the next rep with no hesitation.

A band adds an overspeed eccentric component to power pushups.

Make sure to power breathe—*Tssaa!*—strongly on the top of each swing and pushup rep. This is not only important for maximizing power; this is your ticket to rock-solid abs without adding exercises.

Power Pushup Test

On to testing.

You may do pushups on your palms or fists. Test your pushups after the one-arm swings. Every rep must comply with the SFB standards.

Start the first rep from the bottom, lying prone with your hands on the floor. Brace and explode. Do not cheat with your knees. If your build prevents you from safely going this deep, skip dead starts and do your pushups in the traditional manner starting from the top.

To adjust the pushup resistance, use a rubber band to load or unload, as shown in the next section. Do not elevate your feet or hands.

**Option One
Pushup Accelerometer Test**

This option is ideal.

The test instructions are identical to those for the swing, only instead of changing kettlebells, change the band tension.

If you need to adjust the load with a band, test yourself with several levels of band tension in sets of five with five minutes of rest. Once you have identified the resistance that yields the highest power, do two more sets of five with it with five minutes of rest between them and record the highest reading.

Option Two

Pushup Long Sprint Test

The goal is to find the resistance that allows you to "sprint" for 20–30 seconds.

Your testing partner will count only perfect and explosive reps and must stop the clock earlier than 30 seconds if you are:

- ✓ Losing speed—a repetition takes more time than before
- ✓ Not fully locking out
- ✓ Cutting the ROM on the bottom
- ✓ Losing the plank
- ✓ Resting in the lockout one second or longer

For comparison with future test results, if the timer had to be stopped before 30 seconds, record the time it was stopped.

If you have been unable to sustain high power, high tempo, and impeccable technique for at least 20 seconds, the resistance is too high. Rest for 10 minutes and repeat the test with a band deload.

If, on the other hand, you have completed 30 seconds with high power, rapid-fire cadence, and time to spare, rest for 10 minutes and repeat the test with more resistance.

LOADING AND DELOADING PUSHUPS WITH BANDS

It is tempting to vary the pushup resistance by elevating the feet or hands, but experiments by Fabio Zonin, Master SFG, revealed that this traditional tactic does not work well when pushups are done at max power and high cadence. Without the feedback of a flat ground, people often sag or pike.

Enter the band.

Fabio concluded that looping the band under the pelvis rather than around the chest or armpits is far better for deloading. This point of contact helps the student to fight the tendency to raise the pelvis.

Deloading pushups with a band

Jody Beasley, SFG Team Leader, explains how to go in the opposite direction and load your pushups:

> *These are two similar ways to set up the bands. The only difference between them is where the band rubs against your arms causing some irritation while doing pushups, so it is a personal preference which way to do it. There is minimal difference in resistance.*

Method One

> *Wrap the band around the waist and with palms facing down, insert the thumbs into the looped ends, so the band crosses between the thumb and index finger. Slide the band under the armpits and across the upper back as high as possible. The band should hook across the base of the palms. Be sure to press the hands hard into the floor when performing pushups, actively holding the band down instead of letting it pull against the thumbs.*

Load pushups on fists in the same manner:

Method Two

Wrap the band around the waist and, with the palms facing up, insert the hands into the looped ends hooking the band between the thumb and index finger with it crossing the palm. Slide the band up high around the upper back, passing the elbows through the band, one side going across the back and around the shoulders, the other side crossing the back and passing under the armpits. Be sure to press the hands hard into the floor when performing pushups, actively holding the band down instead of letting it pull against the thumbs.

Before you start loading or deloading, consider this: When you are doing pushups on the floor, you are lifting around 70 percent of your bodyweight.

As you recall, while max power is displayed at about a third to a half of maximal strength, it can be effectively trained with resistance up to 70 percent 1RM. That means a bodyweight bench press is the strength minimum for doing power pushups without a band assist. If you do not bench, 20 strict and slow pushups are an acceptable proxy for a bodyweight bench press.

On the other side of strength, you do not have to band-load your pushups until your bench 1RM exceeds double bodyweight. At that impressive strength level, you are lifting 35 percent 1RM in pushups and are still gaining power.

THE SNATCH: HAIL TSAR!

Did you know that the origin of the Russian word for emperor, "*tsar*," is Latin *Caesar*?

So, hail Tsar! The kettlebell snatch, that is.

KETTLEBELL SNATCH TECHNIQUE

Task:

Kettlebell Snatch

Condition:

Snatch a kettlebell for five repetitions with each arm.

Standard:

1. All of the points that apply to the swing, minus the requirement to keep a straight arm and let the kettlebell float.

2. Swing the kettlebell sitting on the ground in front of you back between your legs and snatch it overhead in one uninterrupted motion into a straight-arm lockout.

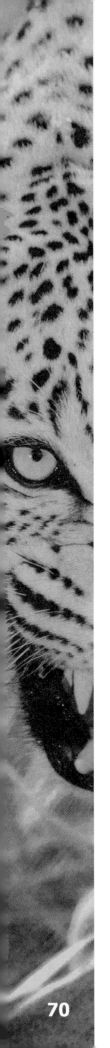

3. Catch the kettlebell softly without banging your forearm or jarring your elbow or shoulder.

4. At the lockout, the arm must be level with the head or behind the head, the neck neutral, and the lower back not hyperextended.

5. Maintain the position briefly, with the arm and legs straight and the feet and body motionless.

6. Actively lower the kettlebell between your legs in one loose, uninterrupted motion close to the body, without touching the chest or shoulder, and snatch again.

7. Be explosive and practice the biomechanical breathing match (inhale on the way down and forcefully exhale on the way up).

Regardless of your choice of test, repeat it once every four to six weeks, during a session after a minimal volume day (40 reps). Keep your warm-ups consistent, as well as the time of the day you are testing, the rests between sets, the shoes or lack of thereof, etc.

Every rep must comply with the SFG standards.

You may use overspeed eccentrics to the extent you are accustomed to doing them with the chosen weight.

Option One
Snatch Accelerometer Test

If you have access to an accelerometer or a force plate, test yourself snatching different size kettlebells in sets of five, with five minutes of rest between sets, to identify the 'bell that enables maximal power expression. Repeat the test two more times with the same 'bell and record the highest reading.

Option Two

Snatch Long Sprint Test

Identify the kettlebell you can "sprint" with for 20–30 seconds.

In addition to the SFG standards, there are two other rules.

First, setting the kettlebell down or switching hands is not allowed.

Second, the lockout, while strict and legal, must be less than one second in duration.

Test your non-dominant side first. Record only perfect, explosive reps. If you pause in the lockout for one second or longer, stop the test, as the reps after this pause do not count—this test is a sprint.

If you have been unable to sprint snatch for at least 20 seconds with the selected kettlebell, it is too heavy to use in this program. Rest for 10 minutes and repeat the test with a lighter kettlebell. If, on the other hand, you have easily completed 30 seconds with high power, rest for 10 minutes and repeat the test with a heavier kettlebell.

Use chalk generously to make sure grip is not the limiting factor.

After 10 minutes of rest, test your dominant side.

PART IV: HAPPY HUNTING!

CIRCUIT TRAINING, LIMITED

Your Q&D protocol is a circuit made up of two exercises: swings and power pushups.

After a warm-up of choice, alternate a series of pulls and pushes. There are always 20 reps in a series, made up of either four sets of five reps (5/4) or two sets of 10 reps (10/2).

In one-arm swings, switch arms from set to set: 10L, 10R or 5L, 5R, 5L, 5R.

Rest actively between sets and series. Walk around, do "fast and loose" drills: Swing your limbs like you are shaking water off them.

Within each series, you will be doing a set of five reps every 30 seconds or 10 reps on the minute. The rest between series is the time left until the start of the next minute, plus one minute: around 1:20 with 5/4 and 1:45 with 10/2.

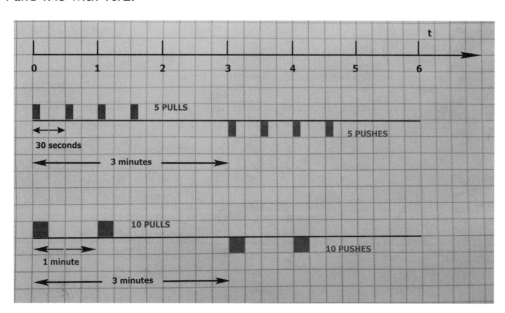

Here is how this works for 10/2.

When the timer starts at 00:00, do a set of 10 pulls with your left arm. Rest actively for the rest of the first minute. At 01:00, do a second set of 10 pulls, this time with your right.

After the set, the clock shows around 01:15. Rest for the remainder of the minute, plus another full minute. When the timer shows 03:00, start a series of pushes.

Note that every pushup rep must start from the ground—exactly as during the test.

Here is how this works for 5/4.

When the timer starts at 00:00, do a set of five pulls with your left arm. Rest actively until 00:30 and do another set of five, this time with your right. Then, do five left at 01:00 and five right at 01:30.

You have just completed a series of 5/4 and the clock shows about 01:40. Rest for the remainder of the minute, plus another full minute. When the timer shows 03:00, start an identical series of pushes.

Thus, a single circuit of one series of each exercise (20 reps), plus the rest intervals between them, takes six minutes. Each session has two to five such circuits: 12, 18, 24, and 30 minutes, minus some change. Your average session is just over 20 minutes long.

Here is how the above template applies to a single exercise, the snatch.

Instead of alternating sets or series of two drills, left- and right-hand snatches are treated as separate events. In one series, you do 20 total reps with the left; in the next one, do them with the right.

The only difference from the swing and pushup template is an extra minute of rest between series. In the single kettlebell snatch, while one side of the lower body works harder than the other, the latter does not exactly chill. Thus, each series—work plus rest—is four minutes long rather than three.

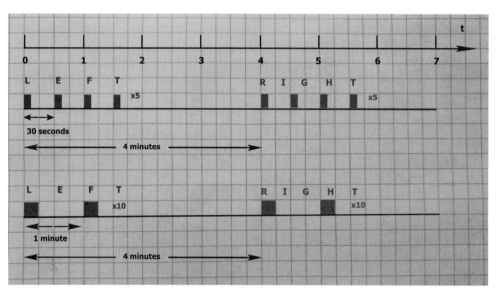

Snatches must be performed with maximal power and a high cadence—but with legal lockouts.

After a warm-up of choice, alternate the series done with your left and right arms. There are always 20 reps in a series, made up of either four sets of five reps (5/4) or two sets of 10 reps (10/2).

Use only one arm in each series:

- Series One: 5L, 5L, 5L, 5L
- Series Two: 5R, 5R, 5R, 5R

Or:

- Series One: 10L, 10L
- Series Two: 10R, 10R

Rest actively between sets and series. Walk around, do "fast and loose" drills. Do not insert other exercises into the rest periods.

Within each series, you will be doing a set of five reps every 30 seconds or 10 reps on the minute. The rest between series is the time left until the start of the next minute, plus two more minutes.

Here is how this works for 10/2.

When the timer starts at 00:00, do a set of 10 pulls with your left arm. Rest actively for the rest of the first minute. At 01:00, do a second set of ten, still with your left.

After the set, the clock shows about 01:20. Rest for the remainder of the minute, plus two full minutes. When the timer shows 04:00, start an identical series with your right.

Here is how this works for 5/4.

When the timer starts at 00:00, do a set of five pulls with your left arm. Rest actively until 00:30 and do another set of five with the left. Then, do five left at 01:00 and another five left at 01:30.

You have just completed a series of 5/4 and the clock shows around 01:40. Rest for the remainder of the minute, plus two full minutes. When the timer shows 04:00, start a series with your right.

The above work-to-rest ratio appears unreasonably generous. Do not compress the rest periods under any circumstances! If you think it is too easy, just add power.

A single series with one arm (20 reps) plus the rest interval before the next series takes four minutes. Each session is made up of two to five such series. This is eight to twenty minutes, ladies and gentlemen, minimalism at its extreme.

This tactic of treating left and right as separate exercises can be applied to swings as well once you have been around the 033 block. Mark, one of the special operators I introduced earlier, did 044 with swings half a year after his experience with 033:

> I just got back from three weeks of Alpine training. It was a typical situation where some guys came up to me at work on a Thursday and asked if I wanted to go climb a mountain on Sunday. No training or preparation.

> The third day I was at the mountain, I did a 10-mile cross-country ski at altitude. I hadn't done backcountry skiing in eight years and am at a low level of proficiency. I honestly believe the only reason I survived it and those after is because I had been doing the 044 template the four weeks prior. My posterior chain was strong and conditioned to get me up the hills and my core was solid to keep me tight while I was tired as hell and had to go down some rough slopes.

WHERE IS THE CARDIO?

Do not compress the rest periods under any circumstances!

You might argue that you have seen people put up impressive power with much less rest. How about the ladies and gents who have completed Sinister, 10/10 in five minutes with 32kg and 48kg, respectively?

Apples and oranges. Their power is impressive by anyone's standards—except their own. At the five-minute mark, SFG Team Leader Roxanne Myers' 100th swing might be more powerful than most men's rep number one—but it pales next to her own number one. S&S is a different program, built according to different specs. It cannot guide the Q&D rests, or vice versa.

Roxanne Myers, SFG Team Leader went beyond Sinister with 10x10 one-arm swings in 5min with 36kg.

"Changing the rest intervals...within a training session enables eliciting totally different biochemical reactions to the identical total load..." warned Prof. Yakovlev.

Given the generous rest periods demanded by the desired adaptations within the working muscles, you might be tempted to sneak in another drill or two that work some muscles relatively untouched by the two main events.

Do not.

Artists have a term, *horror vacui*, that describes the fear of empty space. This phobia applies to program design every bit as it does to that of a room or a painting composition. Do not be a programming pack rat. A third exercise is a gateway drug that will lead you to abandon minimalism and start doing leg presses, lunges, external shoulder rotations with soup cans while sitting on a foam roller...and possibly Pilates.

Seriously, you have only so much nerve force to put out in one session. Our experiments have shown that 200 total reps of max power exercise (100 pulls plus 100 pushes) are all an experienced athlete can handle with top quality.

Sure, you could do some other stuff right after—strength, aerobic endurance, etc.—but you are done with speed and power for the day.

Since Q&D is a circuit, one might think that one of its goals is "cardio," VO_2 max, oxygen transport, heart and lungs, or whatever else you call it.

Sort of. There is enough work to meet the cardiovascular exercise requirements set by government health bodies—but not more. This is why you will find it strange when you end up doing not too shabby in an endurance challenge.

Senior SFG instructor Derek Toshner reported after another killer performance in the TSC five-minute snatch with a 32kg kettlebell:

> *I am definitely keeping the [Q&D] snatch program you sent. I felt like my cardio wasn't there, yet somehow I still snuck out 137 reps. I felt very strong.*

There are multiple factors in play. Bigger and better mitochondria are front and center. Russian scientist Andrey Antonov calculated that a regular untrained adult's heart pumps out enough oxygen to enable him to keep up with advanced runners in a long-distance race.

> *Then why does he not [keep up]…and, moreover, gets out of breath climbing to the third floor? Because his muscles have few mitochondria…Without mitochondria, a muscle cannot utilize oxygen. The heart delivers enough oxygen to the muscles to run at a Master of Sport level, but the remaining oxygen is wasted.*

While we do not yet know how to fully develop our mitochondria to the point where they vacuum up and use all the incoming oxygen, the point has been made.

Scientists used to believe that the VO_2 max was the bottleneck and the end-all of elite endurance performance. Today's prevailing point of view is that it is the muscles' ability to extract arriving oxygen and utilize it in the mitochondria that limits further growth of results and thus must be the training priority.

Thus spake Verkhoshansky.

Of course, it does not mean that oxygen transport is irrelevant. If you aim high in an endurance sport like cross-country skiing, you will have to train it. Just do yourself a favor and stay away from "Tabatas" and other pop-HIIT. Why? That we will discuss some other time. Stick with the VO_2 max training methods proven at the highest echelons of your sport.

THE DELTA 20 PRINCIPLE

Everyone is familiar with the concept of *progressive overload*. Tomorrow you will lift more weight, do more reps, or get the same work done in less time than yesterday. Next week, the volume, intensity, or density will be higher than this week...and so on and so forth. Although periodic deloads are taken—light and medium days, easier weeks, a brand-new 12-week cycle—the overall pattern of progression is straight as an arrow.

An alternative training principle, *variable overload,* was developed by Prof. Arkady Vorobyev:

Both non-organic and organic nature is characterized by the so-called step-like function change. Conversion of chemical energy into mechanical, electromagnetic, and thermal energy also happens stepwise. Discrete changes on sub-cellular and cellular levels are most likely one of the characteristics of live organisms. Although not excluding the principle of gradual overload [over a longer term], we propose sudden yet fitting the given athlete's functional abilities changes in load—'jumps.' This principle of organizing the training loads allows one to achieve higher results with a smaller loading volume.

Prof. Arkady Vorobyev, one of the greatest sports scientists in history—not to mention, a twenty-time world record holder and a two-time Olympic champion in weightlifting.

Soviet weightlifters and, decades later, Russian powerlifters saw spectacular results from variable overload. At StrongFirst we developed Plan Strong™, a general strength training system faithfully adapted from the Soviet weightlifting methodology that produced records that still stand.

"Perhaps the principle of variability applies only to strength sports?" inquires Prof. Vorobyev. "As it turns out, no. [Experiments] convincingly proved that this principle has a significantly larger effect on the increase of athletic results, compared to other methods of load organization, in track and field, swimming, and gymnastics...The principle of variable load organization is applicable to athletes of any sport and any qualification."

We applied elements of Plan Strong™ programming to Strong Endurance™ training protocols with great success. The key is the Delta 20 Principle. It means that a minimum volume change from one training unit to the next is 20 percent. Thus, "Δ 20 %" or "Delta 20."

Compared to the baby steps practiced in progressive overload, variable overload volume whiplashes up and down with Δ 20 percent as a rock-bottom minimum—and Δ 100 percent and higher on a regular basis. This shocks the system with expectedly superior performance gains—and, as Prof. Vorobyev's research revealed, unexpectedly better wellbeing.

Fabio Zonin, Master SFG teaching a Plan Strong™ seminar

Given the Q&D mandate to maintain max power, the regimen is treated as a power regimen. Variable overload is a perfect match for power training, where progressive overload makes no sense at all. You are already giving each rep 100 percent, so there is nowhere to go up, at least in the short term. Your resistance has been optimized for max power production, so increasing it would be counterproductive. It could be varied, but, as the word implies, that is variability rather than progression. Increasing the reps per set or the number of sets would compromise the power and unrecognizably alter the metabolic events and the resulting adaptations.

In summary, while you will see power go up over weeks and the weight enabling max power increase over months, there is no short-term progression, only practice and variability.

The perfect parameter to vary on the Q&D protocol is the daily volume, the rep total.

We already know the top end: 100 reps. How low can we go and what other options will there be between the high and the low?

The answers are 40, 60, 80, and 100.

These numbers were picked for several reasons.

First, they are multiples of 20—the number of reps per series.

Second, any two consecutive numbers guarantee a minimal volume change of 20 percent (from 100 to 80), with the delta shooting much higher in other combinations, all the way up to 150 percent (from 40 to 100).

Third, students of Plan Strong™ who choose to dismantle these digits will recognize that they hit the bull's eye of Prof. Anatoly Chernyak's "magic numbers" or *stable structural constants*.

Great news for programming simplicity: In the Q&D context these numbers can be arranged in any order.

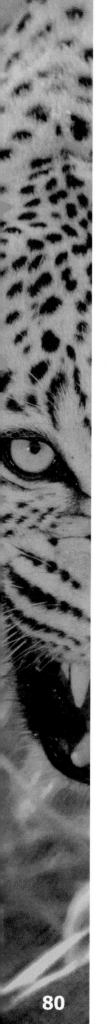

Traditional athletic training periodization calls for a *preparatory period* and a *competition period*. The former builds stable long-term adaptations in strength, endurance, and other qualities. The latter does not build anything, but creates the perfect short-term conditions to realize the potential built in the prep period.

If one is peaking for a given date, the order in which the "magic numbers" are arranged must follow special formulae. But in the prep period, any order works.

And for the purposes of many Q&D readers, peaking is irrelevant—at least in the Q&D drills.

In the early 2000s, I introduced variable overload within the context of *tactical periodization* to special operations teams I was working with as a subject matter expert.

Traditional periodization involves long-term planning and peaking on a given day. Both are out for a deployed serviceman and, more recently, servicewoman. On any given day, bad guys may have some ideas other than a heavy squat.

In contrast, *tactical periodization* is short-term training planning that emphasizes sharp and near-random variation of the training load. In other words, it is Prof. Vorobyev's sharp variability adapted to highly kinetic environments.

Of course, war is not the only such environment. Less dramatic but equally unpredictable are a suburban house full of kids or a start-up campus. Hence, most adults should model their training on that of warriors rather than athletes.

To introduce more randomness within our strictly defined load parameters, you will be rolling a die to determine the rep count for each of your three weekly Q&D sessions.

Note that you will always be doing an identical number of reps in both exercises: 40+40, 100+100, etc. In the one-arm swings, count the sum of both arms. For example, on the day with 40 reps, you will do 10L, 10R, 10L, 10R.

Here is how it works with swings and pushups.

SWING + PUSHUP					
Total daily reps per exercise (in one-arm swings, the sum of both arms)					
Die shows	1	2	3	4	5	6
Total reps	40	60		80		100
Number of series	2	3		4		5
Session duration	12 min	18 min		24 min		30 min
If you rolled the same rep count as the last session, roll again.					
If you are having an off day, do not roll a die. Instead, do two series (40 reps) for each lift.					

Of course, occasionally, when circumstances insist, you may choose not to roll a die and simply pick the daily volume most suitable to what happened yesterday or what is about to happen later today or tomorrow. Just do not make a habit of it, as your bias toward some numbers would reduce the randomness and thus the effectiveness of the method.

A word about days when you are supposed to train, but you just do not have max intensity in you: Do a minimal volume session of 40 reps, but do not go full power. Relax and keep your effort dial at around three-quarters of max. You will still net many benefits from such a session, one being the ability to learn to minimize counterproductive tension in antagonistic muscles. This applies to both swing plus pushup and snatch loads.

The snatch variability is the same, but the length of a training session is two-thirds of that of swings plus pushups:

SNATCH						
Total daily reps, sum of both arms						
Die shows	1	2	3	4	5	6
Total reps	40	60		80		100
Number of series	2	3		4		5
Session duration	8 min	12 min		16 min		20 min
If you rolled the same rep count as the last session, roll again.						
If you are having an off day, do not roll a die. Instead, do two series (40 reps).						

Note that on days with three and five series, you start and finish with your non-dominant side, thus giving it 20 extra reps. Try not to let this drive you crazy.

Once you have established the daily volume, roll a die to set the daily set and rep scheme:

SWING + PUSHUP						
Reps and Sets within Series						
Die shows	1	2	3	4	5	6
Reps/sets	5/4		Alternate series of 5/4 and 10/2[6]		10/2	
If you are having an off day, do not roll a die. Instead, do 5/4 for both lifts.						

SNATCH						
Reps and Sets within Series						
Die shows	1	2	3	4	5	6
Reps/sets	5/4		Alternate series of (5L/4) + (5R/4) and (10L/2) + (10R/2)[7]		10/2	
If you are having an off day, do not roll a die. Instead, do 5/4.						

---

[6] As an example, the day calls for 60 reps per exercise. Do SW (5/4), P (5/4), SW (10/2), P (10/2), SW (5/4), P (5/4).

[7] (5L/4), (5R/4); (10L/2), (10R/2). Note that on days with three and five series, the load for your left and right arms will not be identical.

Finally, choose the swing variation:

Swing Type						
Die shows	1	2	3	4	5	6
Swing type	Two-arm			One-arm		

If you are equally comfortable pushing up on your palms and fists, you may add an additional degree of variability by rolling a die between the two:

Pushup Type						
Die shows	1	2	3	4	5	6
Pushup Type	Palms			Fists		

In the snatch, there is no specialized variety. The minimalism is ultimate: one drill, one version.

Variable overload is one of the most powerful programming tools in existence. It enables us to meet two contradicting requirements: specificity and novelty. And the above die-driven algorithms are a foolproof way to implement this highly sophisticated training system.

BUILT TO LAST

There are times when an athlete is forced to cut way back on training or even stop altogether.

And not just an athlete. A Marine deployed into harm's way. A sleep-deprived parent. An entrepreneur.

Aimed at a reader living a life full of sharp turns, Q&D was designed to minimize deconditioning during layoffs. Here is how.

First, the Q&D endurance resides in the mitochondria and is not limited by cardio. VO_2 max is one of the first markers to go to pot when you stop training—especially if you have been doing intervals rather than steady-state training. And, unfairly, the higher your VO_2 max, the steeper its decline.

Second, what was built persists longer than what has been pumped up.

"Brick and mortar" morphological adaptations are far more stable than biochemical ones. Compare the shelf life of muscle mass grown with different methods. A bodybuilder starts losing size days after leaving the gym. Muscle glycogen stores rapidly shrink from disuse and, since one molecule of glycogen binds three molecules of water, his pipes lose their pumped-up look. In contrast, a powerlifter may take a month off and those guns will hardly show it. It takes the "real" muscle—the myofibrils—an entire month of laziness before they start wilting.

By the same token, the Q&D endurance that relies on increased mitochondrial mass will outlast the metcon endurance dependent on fickle glycogen stores, glycolytic enzymes, and acid buffers.

Third, what is built slowly will outlast what was slapped together.

Think of a cathedral erected over decades of loving labor versus a house mass produced without pride in one's craftsmanship. The former will outlast the latter by centuries.

The longer the training period, the deeper the adaptations and the more resistant they are to detraining. Soviet scientists made two groups of subjects stop training for 30 days. Before this layoff, one group had trained for 30 days and the other for 90 days. Following a month of laziness, the oxidative capacity in the first "get fit quick" group reverted back to the pre-training levels...like their training never happened. In contrast, the group that put their time in the gym experienced no decrease at all.

Q&D was meant to be practiced for months and years, not weeks.

Fourth, Q&D's fixation on power enables the athlete to retain all fitness qualities during times of reduced training.

Soviets discovered that the greater the speed component in low-volume maintenance loads, the more pronounced their detraining prevention effects. "This opens up opportunities for using special low volume loads for maintaining athletes' training level in situations when the athlete is forced to stop full volume training for one reason or another," comments Prof. Yakovlev. This is yet another reason to be "fast first."

Fifth, the rate of future detraining can be slowed by decreasing today's training frequency.

During the Cold War, German scientists discovered that the more frequently we train, the quicker we detrain—and vice versa. Hence, skipping an occasional week or longer will be less punishing to performance if we normally train twice a week.

Q&D offers an option of training only twice a week. Although training daily favors mitochondrial adaptations, twice a week is enough to make excellent gains, as witnessed by the earlier-mentioned repeat sprint experiment with advanced wrestlers. There is a mountain of evidence that training twice a week is sufficient for power, and for muscle hypertrophy as well.

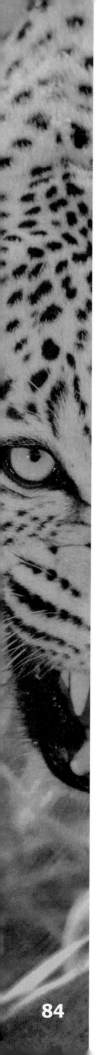

THE SCHEDULE

Twice a week is good and three are better.

In many types of training, twice-a-week frequency is the minimal effective dose, with four times a week being the point of diminishing returns. Hence, the Q&D choice is three times a week, where effectiveness meets efficiency—the timeless Monday, Wednesday, and Friday schedule.

On to your Q&D day.

Given the brief and energizing nature of Q&D sessions, it is easy to fit it with other types of training. Just remember not to do anything right before it. Fast first.

Q&D after a warm-up of choice. Do the bare minimum recommended by your health care professional plus whatever else you need to stay healthy. Although a much more extensive warm-up increases performance in power exercises (but not strength exercises), it is hard to justify for an ultra-minimalist.

For instance, here is my personal warm-up before Q&D swings and parallel bar dips:

- Assume a wide stance, about two shoulder widths, with the toes turned out more than 45 degrees, and squat to slightly below parallel. Stay there, "pull the hips out of their sockets" and pry for around 10 seconds.
- Stand facing away from a vertical pole. Clasp the hands around the pole, behind the back at the waist level. Lean forward, spread the collarbones, and force the chest open, readying for the bottom of the dip. That was another 10 seconds.
- A couple of hip circles, focusing on the extension—the final 10 seconds.

A grand total of half a minute; make it a whopping full minute if you count the transitions. Boom, I am ready.

I am not suggesting you emulate the above highly individualized routine. I have trained without warm-ups for decades. This is not for everybody.

Train fresh.

The best time of the day depends on your top priority.

For power, do Q&D in the early evening, just not close to bedtime. This protocol spikes your energy and you will have a hard time falling asleep after it.

For health and endurance, do Q&D fasted in the morning.

I am appalled at myself for having broken my decades-long policy of not giving out nutrition advice, but this message was too persistent in mitochondrial research to ignore.

As discussed in the earlier section on ATP, AMPK measures not just AMP, but other manifestations of low energy. As such, AMPK is not as readily activated by training if you are fed like a bodybuilder or stocked with glycogen like a marathoner. This is why Q&D training is most effective in the morning in a fasted state.

Obviously, sipping some ridiculous "energy drink" before or during a training session would inhibit the effects of your training on the mitochondria.

And even after. Research suggests that ideally, to reinforce the message, you should stay fasted for a while after stimulating mitochondria with training. How long is a personal compromise based on many factors. Obviously, delaying feeding the cat compromises hypertrophy and glycogen replenishment.

When you start Q&D, do not jump into the full load, but build up to it over a couple of weeks. The first week, accept only 40 and 60 reps—roll again if the die assigns you more. The second week, accept 80, but still deny 100. After that, you should be good to go with a full load.

The first week, do exclusively the 5/4 series. The second week, start rolling a die, but limit your choices to 5/4 and alternating 5/4 and 10/2. From the third week forward, anything goes.

Hold back your power to 80–90 percent for the first week or two, then go full throttle.

Early on, swing or snatch with a free fall. Once you can comfortably do your 100 total reps with max power, ease into overspeed eccentrics. "Whatever you do, do not overestimate your capabilities," warned Dr. Mel Siff. "Remember that this is really a type of 'supramaximal' force training and it can impose extremely large stresses on your soft tissues."

Start lightly accelerating the 'bell on the way down and back. Build up very slowly until any of the following occurs:

- ✓ You sense that adding even more power on the way down might cause injury.
- ✓ You know that your skin on your palms will not be able to take a more violent deceleration.
- ✓ You are unable to throw the 'bell down and back any faster.

At this point, retest your power; it is almost certainly time to move up in weight.

To reinforce the point about being gradual when picking up the downward acceleration, here is the formula of kinetic energy:

$$KE = (mv^2) / 2$$

Kinetic energy carried by an object in motion is directly proportional to its mass multiplied by the square of its velocity. Double the mass of a bullet and you will double its destructive potential. Double its speed—and its lethal energy will quadruple.

Q&D, the Summary: Swings and Pushups

Q&D is an advanced, minimalist, self-contained GPP platform that develops a wide range of qualities, with the emphasis on power, while minimizing fatigue and soreness and leaving plenty of time and energy for other pursuits.

WHEN TO TRAIN

Train two or three times a week.

Train fresh.

The best time of the day to train depends on your top priority.

• For power, train Q&D in the early evening, but not close to bedtime.

• For health and endurance, train Q&D fasted in the morning.

TRAINING SESSION ORGANIZATION

Do Q&D after a warm-up of choice.

Pulls and pushes must be performed with maximal power, a high cadence, and total compliance with the SFG and SFB technique standards.

Do not lose the float in swings or full lockouts in pushups!

After a warm-up of choice, alternate series of pulls and pushes. There are always 20 reps in a series, made up of either four sets of five reps (5/4) or two sets of 10 reps (10/2).

In one-arm swings, switch arms from set to set: 10L, 10R or 5L, 5R, 5L, 5R.

Rest actively between sets and series. Walk around, do "fast and loose" drills.

Within each series, you will be doing a set of five reps every 30 seconds or 10 reps on the minute. The rest between series is the time left until the start of the next minute, plus one minute: around 1:20 with 5/4 and about 1:45 with 10/2.

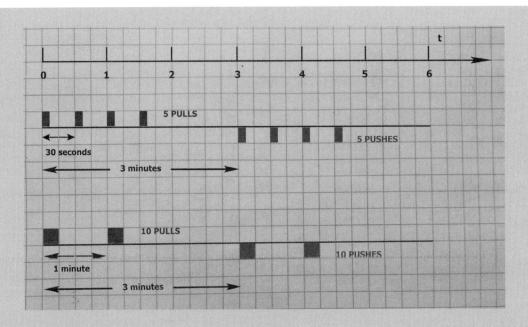

Do not compress the rest periods under any circumstances! If you think it is too easy, add power.

TRAINING SESSION LOAD

Roll a die to determine the load parameters.

Step One: Session Volume

The number of series of one exercise is two to five (40–100 total reps). In one-arm swings, count the sum of both arms.

Do the same number of series in both drills, always starting with swings. Roll a die to determine the daily volume:

Die shows	1	2	3	4	5	6
Total reps	40	60		80		100
Number of series	2	3		4		5
Session duration	12 min	18 min		24 min		30 min
If you rolled the same rep count as the last session, roll again.						

If you are having an off day, do not roll a die. Instead, do two series (40 reps) for each lift.

Step Two: Reps and Sets within Series

Die shows	1	2	3	4	5	6
Reps/sets	5/4		Alternate series of 5/4 and 10/2		10/2	

If you are having an off day, do not roll a die, but do 5/4 for both lifts.

Step Three: Swing Type

Die shows	1	2	3	4	5	6
Swing type	Two-arm			One-arm		

Step Four: Pushup Type (Optional)

Die shows	1	2	3	4	5	6
Pushup Type	Palms			Fists		.

Q&D, THE SUMMARY: SNATCHES

Q&D is an advanced, minimalist, self-contained GPP platform that develops a wide range of qualities, with the emphasis on power while minimizing fatigue and soreness and leaving plenty of time and energy for other pursuits.

WHEN TO TRAIN

Train two or three times a week.

Train fresh.

The best time of the day depends on your top priority.

- For power, train Q&D in the early evening, but not close to bedtime.

- For health and endurance, train Q&D fasted in the morning.

TRAINING SESSION ORGANIZATION

Do Q&D after a warm-up of choice.

Snatches must be performed with maximal power, a high cadence, and total compliance with the SFG technique standards. **Do not smudge the lockout!**

Left and right snatches are treated as separate events. In one series, do your 20 total reps with the left…in the next one, with the right.

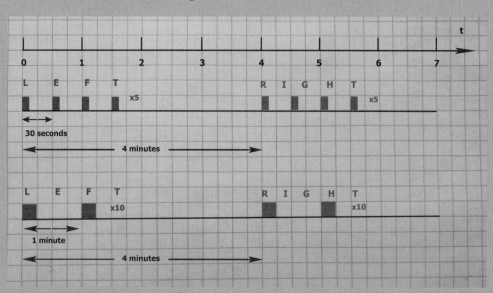

After a warm-up of choice, alternate series done with your left and right arm. There are always 20 reps in a series, made up of either four sets of five reps (5/4) or two sets of 10 reps (10/2).

Use only one arm in each series:

- Series One: 5L, 5L, 5L, 5L
- Series Two: 5R, 5R, 5R, 5R

Or:

- Series One: 10L, 10L
- Series Two: 10R, 10R

Rest actively between sets and series. Walk around, do "fast and loose" drills. Do not insert other exercises into the rest periods.

Within each series, you will be doing a set of five reps every 30 seconds or 10 reps on the minute. The rest between series is the time left until the start of the next minute, plus two more minutes.

Do not compress the rest periods under any circumstances! If you think it is too easy, add power.

A single series with one arm (20 reps) plus the rest interval before the next series takes four minutes. Each session is made up of two to five such series, for a total of eight to 20 minutes.

TRAINING SESSION LOAD

Roll a die to determine the load parameters.

Step One: Session Volume

Count the sum of both arms.

Die shows	1	2	3	4	5	6
Total reps	40	60		80		100
Number of series	2	3		4		5
Session duration	8 min	12 min		16 min		20 min
If you rolled the same rep count as the last session, roll again.						

Note that on days with three and five series, you start and finish with your non-dominant side, thus giving it 20 extra reps.

If you are having an off day, do not roll a die, but do two series (40 reps).

Step Two: Reps and Sets within Series

Die shows	1	2	3	4	5	6
Reps/sets	5/4		Alternate series of (5L/4) + (5R/4) and (10L/2) + (10R/2)		10/2	

If you are having an off day, do not roll a die, but do 5/4.

Each Chooses for Oneself

How long should you stay on Q&D before moving on to a compatible training method like A+A[8]?

Ideally, three months.

Within the first six weeks, mitochondrial and myofibrillar adaptations are most pronounced. Dedicate the second six weeks to owning your new power and conditioning.

Can you stay on Q&D longer than 12 weeks?

Yes. We have had some athletes, including pros, Q&D successfully for many months. High-variability loads postpone plateaus, as discovered by Prof. Vorobyev.

But even with the Delta 20 Principle in your corner, eventually the rate of progress will diminish. Be content maintaining your performance at a high level with a minimal time and energy investment. Or keep gains coming by introducing additional types of variability into Q&D.

Vary the Training Days

One type of variability is to change the training days within a week. If you are not one of those hyper-organized types who goes insane at a hint of asymmetry—the vase must be exactly in the center of the table!—instead of the traditional Monday/Wednesday/Friday schedule, toss a coin or roll a die.

Early Soviet coaching was driven by Pavlov's teaching that one adapts best "when certain stimuli are repeated in a strict order and with strict intervals between them." In the 1960s, the Soviets still considered high regularity of training an asset. Then Prof. Vorobyev came along and concluded that while a Monday/Wednesday/Friday rhythm is nice for beginners, it is suboptimal for experienced athletes whose systems need more surprises, at least outside the competition period.

Take Saturdays or Sundays off. Toss a coin or roll a die every remaining day of the week.

Am I Training Today?		
Coin shows	Heads	Tails
Die shows	1, 2, 3	4, 5, 6
Training	Yes	No

---

[8] "A+A" or "alactic plus aerobic" training is a classic form of Soviet anti-glycolytic training. Read about it in the articles section on StrongFirst.com.

A very effective strategy to take after the first 12-week run of Q&D is alternating six-week phases of Q&D and A+A. Both develop the fast-fiber mitochondria, albeit in different ways. Both train the power and net many WTHEs. If combined with other types of variability listed in this chapter, this strategy is likely to be sustainable for years.

You will end up with a long-term average of the same number of sessions a week. The cool thing —and maddening for some—is the bizarre way this average will be arrived at. For humor's sake I flipped a coin for 12 weeks. Enjoy your variability.

Sample 12 Q&D Weeks with Variable Training Days								
Week	**Mon**	**Tue**	**Wed**	**Thur**	**Fri**	**Sat**	**Sun**	**Total**
I	+				+	+		3
II	+		+			+		3
III			+			+		2
IV	+		+		+			3
V			+		+			2
VI			+					1
VII	+		+		+		Off	3
VIII		+				+		2
IX	+				+			2
X		+	+	+	+	+		5
XI					+			1
XII	+					+		2

That said, few people can afford the luxury of such randomness for professional, athletic, and social reasons. It is okay to stick with the boring old Monday/Wednesday/Friday.

VARY THE EXERCISES

Make the exercise selection more variable. For instance, do swings plus pushups on some days and snatches on others. You could lean toward the former for one month:

Die shows	1	2	3	4	5	6
Exercises	Swings and pushups			Snatches		

…and toward the latter the next month:

Die shows	1	2	3	4	5	6
Exercises	Snatches			Swings and pushups		

If you know what you are doing, you could introduce more specialized variety. For example, replace swings with jump squats or side walking swings on some days.

Vary the Resistance

You might also introduce resistance variability.

Stay biased toward the weight or band tension that enables max power or one a bit heavier, but periodically go a fifth to a third heavier. This is simple with kettlebells, less so with bands, manageable with a backpack.

Power pushups with a weighted vest

Half the reps per set, from 10 to four or six; from five to two or three. Cut enough repetitions to make sure your swings do not turn into what former Master SFG instructor Jeff O'Connor called "fast grinds"—not even on the last set of a max volume session of five series.

For instance, if your max power weight is 32kg and you have been doing 32kg x 5/4 and 32kg x 10/2, on heavy days lift 40kg x 2–3/4 or 40kg x 4–6/2. In other words, your loads with 32kg were four sets of five on some days and two sets of 10 on others. With 40kg, you will be doing four sets of doubles or triples or two sets of four to six reps.

You can vary the resistance from day to day or within a session.

Again, stay partial toward your max power weight. Let us call it "X." You might decide to draw up a table similar to the one below that removes the guesswork from the weight selection on a given day:

Die shows	1	2	3	4	5	6
Weight	X + (20–33%)			X		

Naturally, you can do the same for banded pushups, although you will have to do some guesswork with percentages.

An occasional detour into lighter resistance—less frequent than heavy work—would not hurt either. Speed training has a carryover to power.

Resistance as light as 15–20 percent of max resistance is used in Russia for training speed and frequency of unloaded movements. For the sake of simplicity, subtract the same 20–33 percent from your "X" max power 'bell.

Up the reps per set by 50 percent: from 10 to 15; from five to seven or eight. For instance, if you have been doing 32kg x 5/4 and 32kg x 10/2 as your standard "X" load, when you go lighter, swing 24kg x 7/2, 8/2 and 24kg x 15/2.

Here is a sample table introducing speed loads into your Q&D regimen:

Die shows	1	2	3	4	5	6
Weight	X - (20–33%)	X + (20–33%)		X		

An advanced practitioner may choose to add a band to the two-arm swing for an overspeed eccentric extra kick. Use a light kettlebell. Take in moderation.

Up the Volume, Kill the Variability

For a couple of months, switch to the most streamlined version of Q&D, formerly "StrongFirst Experimental Plan 015."

Do 10x10 in both exercises, each every three minutes. When the timer starts at 00:00, do a set of 10 swings with your left arm. At 01:30, do 10 pushups. At 03:00, 10 swings with your right. At 04:30, 10 pushups, etc. You may have recognized the protocol used by "Victor."

Train at least three times a week. If you recover well, go up to four and even five.

Although this type of loading is less effective than 033 in some ways—less CP depletion and no variability whatsoever—it more than makes up for it in other ways.

You should put on some mass. The Soviet weightlifting national team head coach Robert Roman knew that, "Everything else being equal, an increase in the training volume facilitates a large increase in muscle mass."

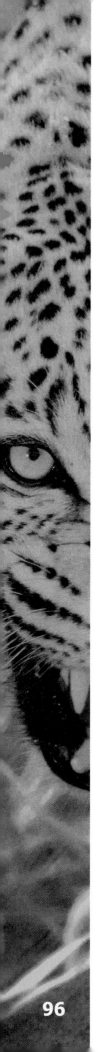

The authoritative Russian military *Encyclopedia of Physical Training* teaches us that both hypertrophy and aerobic training demand less variability than power and strength training. In other words, we can get away with flat-lining the load for awhile.

I witnessed the muscle-building effects of 100 daily power reps when I met a former coach of the Bulgarian national gymnastics team. Old enough to have adult sons, Ivan Ivanov had the physique most 20-year-olds would not even dream to achieve. And still does a decade later.

The choices are yours to make. Per Russian poet Yuri Levitansky:

> *Each chooses for himself*
> *His woman, his faith, and his road.*
> *To serve the Savior or the devil,*
> *Each chooses for himself.*
>
> *Each chooses for himself*
> *The words to love and pray.*
> *The blades to fight*
> *Each chooses for himself.*
>
> *Each chooses for himself*
> *His shield and armor, staff and rags.*
> *The measure of the final penance*
> *Each chooses for himself.*
>
> *Each chooses for himself.*
> *I choose the best I can.*
> *I have no claims to anyone,*
> *Each chooses for himself.*

Epilogue: Animal Supreme

It is fitting to close this book with a big cat quote. In novelist Robert Sheckley's inimitable style:

> He yawned, revealing incisors like Turkish scimitars. He stretched, showing a smooth ripple of muscle down either flank like sluggish octopi grappling beneath a thin sheet of plastic...His tail stood out stiff and straight and high, like the indicator of a dial calibrated for trouble.

Happy hunting!

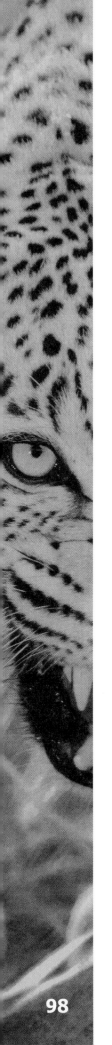

ACKNOWLEDGEMENTS

The author would like to thank the following colleagues for their valuable feedback and suggestions:

Jon Engum, Dr. Steve Freides, John Heinz, Brett Jones, Pavel Macek, Dr. Craig Marker, Peter Park, Mark Reifkind, Phil Scarito, Alexey Senart—and especially Fabio Zonin.

Photo credits:

Leopard (cover and throughout the book): Stuart G Porter/Shutterstock.com
Peter Park and JJ Muno: Courtesy of Peter Park
Barracuda: Rich Carey/Shutterstock.com
Leopard relaxing: Volodymyr Burdiak/Shutterstock.com
Dan Austin and Hideaki Inaba: Courtesy of *Powerlifting USA*
Jaguar fighting caiman: nwdph/Shutterstock.com
Cheetah hunting: Elana Erasmus/Shutterstock.com
Derek Toshner: Lydia Toshner
Roxanne Myers: Courtesy of Roxanne Myers
Fabio Zonin at Plan Strong™ seminar: Craig Marker

Other credits:

Peak power readings chart: Dr. Craig Marker
"Ferocity of life": Quote from a novel by Roger Zelazny
"Animal supreme": Quote from a song by Iron Maiden.

REFERENCES AND NOTES

Most of the Russian references below are not available in English.

PART I: FAST FIRST

FAST FIRST

- High-level Soviet athletes from different sports were subjected to a battery of tests of different qualities. In strength, sprinters came close to weightlifters and gymnasts, while endurance athletes showed low results. Weightlifters and gymnasts performed poorly in endurance tests and sprinters performed well. (Yakovlev, 1983)

- Quote. (Yakovlev, 1974)

- The myosin and maximal tissue respiration rate, percent improvement from the untrained levels under the influence of different types of training, tables. (Yakovlev, 1974, 1983)

- Maximal power is displayed at around a third to a half of maximal strength in a given movement. (Kotz, 1998)

- The greater the speed, the lower the recruitment threshold force for a given motor unit (Gourfinkel et al., 1970; Gidikov, 1975). For a given MU, the recruitment threshold force is lower in ballistic contractions than in ramp or isometric contractions. (Desmedt & Godaux, 1978; Yoneda et al., 1986)

- In healthy weight-trained men, there was a 15.1 percent increase in serum testosterone after 10 sets of five reps of jump squats with 70 percent of the system mass and two-minute rests. (Volek et al., 1985)

- Quote. (Fry & Lohnes, 2010)

- In aging, the dynamic component of strength (jumps, throws, quick lifts) declines first, while static strength declines slower. (Yakovlev, 1983)

- In aging, there is a preferential loss of type II fibers; a sedentary 80-year-old man has lost half the fast fibers he had as a 30-year-old. Quote. (Zatsiorsky & Kraemer, 2006)

- At rest and per pound, 70-year-olds consume 40 percent less oxygen than 20- and 30-year-olds. (Yakovlev, 1983)

- To stimulate both the plastic and the energetic processes in children, teenagers, and the elderly, accelerations are recommended. (Yakovlev, 1983)

- Although speed training improves aerobic oxidation of carbs but not of fats (Yakovlev, 1983), "When training at high speeds, there is a greater decrease in fatty tissue as compared to training at low speeds." (Platonov et al., 2004)

Acid, the Enemy of the Quick

- High lactic acid concentration is the main factor limiting muscular contraction. (Meerson, 1973, 1986)

  - "Acidosis…leads to disruption of nerve cells' activity and a development of defensive inhibition in them, worsening of excitation transmission from the nerve to the muscle." Na^+-K^+ pumps' conductivity to ions is reduced. (Volkov et al., 2000)
  - H^+ inhibits ATPase, both in myosin and calcium pumps, thus compromising both contraction and relaxation. (Mikhailov, 2002)
  - H^+ interferes with Ca^{2+} reaching the troponin/tropomyosin complex. (Brooks & Fahey, 2004)
  - H^+ depresses Ca^{2+} reuptake into the sarcoplasmic reticula.
  - H^+ inhibits CK, glycolytic, and aerobic enzymes.

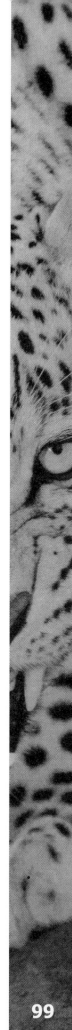

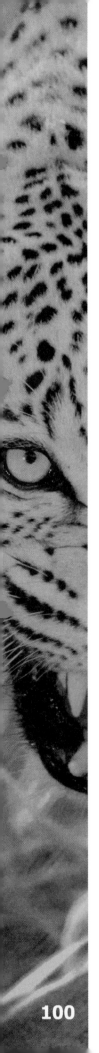

- - H^+ uncouples oxidation and phosphorylation in the mitochondria. (Volkov et al., 2000)

- "Muscle contractility includes parameters such as maximal force, shortening velocity, and a rate of relaxation...Since the power output is the product of force and velocity, a decrease of 20 percent of each of these factors reduces power by almost 40 percent." (Hargreaves & Spriet, 2006)

- Correlation between lactate concentration in the working muscles and the power output decrease graph is based on Volkov et al. (2000).

- In maximal veloergometer exercise power drops by up to 40–50 percent by 30 seconds. (Nevill et al., 1996)

- In the state of fatigue, especially in cyclical work, the muscles no longer able to exert quick, powerful efforts compensate with longer and weaker contractions. (Farfel, 1972; Kourakin, 1972; Volkov et al., 1974) The resulting changes in proprioception and unfavorable metabolic changes lead to a disintegration of the optimal relationships between somatic, vegetative, and other systems, movement discoordination, and a sharp reduction in the working effect of the movement. (Mogendovich, 1963; Mouravov et al., 1984; cited by Verkhoshansky, 1988)

- Study of the anabolic and catabolic effects of different types of exercises and loads in female speedskaters. (Erkomayshvili, 1990)

- Quote. (Selouyanov, 2013)

- An increase of H^+ concentration in the sarcoplasm facilitates the peroxidation reaction. (Hochachka & Somero, 1988) Lower pH makes low activity free radicals convert into more aggressive species. (Hess et al., 1982, etc.)

- In physiologic quantities ROS have a hormetic effect (Yakovlev, 1983): Stimulate synthesis of protective proteins and increases the organism's resistance to stress, exercise, cold, diets rich in oxidative substrates, hypoxia, etc. (Sazontova & Arkhipenko, 2004)

  "The most important physiological functions of ROS include (i) oxidation and utilization of damaged molecules; (ii) synthesis of messenger molecules, and (iii) participation in redox signaling pathways and intracellular transfer of external signals to cell nuclei terminated by protein synthesis..." (Arkhipenko et al., 2014)

  Physiologic concentrations of ROS are essential for initiating mitochondrial biogenesis. (Paulsen et al., 2014) It has been suggested that the expression of PGC-1α requires an optimal concentration of ROS. (Lira et al., 2010)

- There is "a linear relationship between GSSG-to-GSH and lactate-to-pyruvate ratios in human blood before, during, and after exhaustive exercise." (Sastre et al., 1992) GSH is an antioxidant. An increase in the levels of its oxidized version, GSSG, indicates oxidative stress.

The simplified chart in the text, *"Linear relationship between lactate concentration and oxidative stress,"* is based on that by Sastre et al. In the original, the x-axis represents the lactate-to-pyruvate ratio in blood and the y-axis the GSSG-to-GSH ratio.

- ROS are a major destructive factor of morphological structures of muscle fibers. (Pshennikova, 1986)

- It has been suggested that ROS hyper-production in soft and connective tissues and bones may be the cause of degenerative changes, micronecrosis, and loss of elasticity that facilitate injuries. (Tabarchouk et al., 2014)

Adrenaline, the Hormone of Prey

- Peroxidation of lipids (POL) intensifies during stress, regardless of the stress' nature. (Baraboy, 1991) Emotional-pain stress causes activation of POL in the brain and the executive organs (Meerson, 1981); POL concentration goes up two or three-fold. (Prilepko et al., 1983) High doses of catecholamines are accompanied by an increase of POL products in mitochondrial membranes by almost 90 percent. (Swaroop & Ramasarma, 1981)

- "Adrenergic stimulation decreases [antioxidant] GSH synthesis." (Estrella et al., 1988)

- The adrenaline/noradrenaline hypothesis of fear and anger (Funkenstein, 1955) "is a good but not an exhaustive hypothesis to account for the characteristics of the respective autonomic responses." (Potegal et al., 2010)

- Adrenaline-to-noradrenaline ratios in different species. (von Euler, cited in Green, 1987; Rome & Bell, 1983)

- Social animals, domestic and wild, have a high adrenaline-to-noradrenaline ratio. (Reed, 1958)

- A creative "high" that increases physical and mental work capacity is accompanied by noradrenaline secretion. (Yakovlev, 1974)

- Adrenaline and noradrenaline appear to be is associated with, respectively, uncertainty and certainty of outcome. (Kety, cited in McNaughton, 1989)

The Quick and the Dead

- "Whereas a trained athlete can recover from a 100-meter sprint in 30 minutes or less, an alligator may require many hours of rest and extra oxygen consumption to clear the excess lactate from its blood and regenerate muscle glycogen after a burst of activity... Dinosaurs and other huge, now-extinct animals probably had to depend on lactic acid fermentation to supply energy for muscular activity, followed by very long recovery periods during which they were vulnerable to attack by smaller predators better able to use oxygen and better adapted to continuous, sustained muscular activity." (Nelson & Cox, 2012)

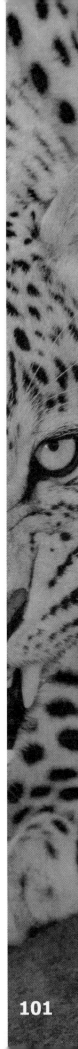

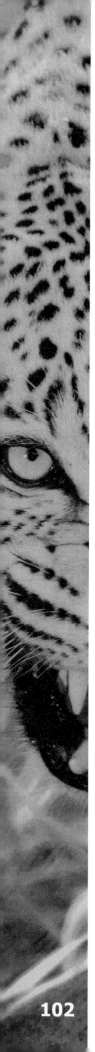

- Quote. (Lane, 2010)

- Adaptation to muscular activity may be accompanied by adaptation to other stimuli: hypoxia, heat, cold, etc. (Rousin, 1984) Competition for oxygen unites these cross adaptations (Platonov et al., 2004) and many take place in the mitochondria (Yakovlev, 1974).

  "For all the differences introduced by the specificity of the stimuli (cold, hypoxia, intense muscle work, etc.), the adaptation mechanism is characterized by pronounced generality (Meerson, 1973; Kaznacheev, 1980)…the same change takes place in cells of many physiological systems—a deficit of energy rich phosphate compounds and an increase in phosphorylation potential. This activates the cells' genetic apparatus, intensifying synthesis of nucleic acids and proteins." (Verkhoshansky, 1985)

- "The metabolic role of mitochondria is so critical to cellular and organismal function that defects in mitochondrial function have very serious medical consequences. Mitochondria are central to neuronal and muscular function, and to the regulation of whole-body energy metabolism and body weight. Human neurodegenerative diseases, as well as cancer, diabetes, and obesity, are recognized as possible results of compromised mitochondrial function, and one theory of aging is based on a gradual loss of mitochondrial integrity. ATP production is not the only important mitochondrial function; this organelle also acts in thermogenesis, steroid synthesis, and apoptosis (programmed cell death)." (Nelson & Cox, 2012)

- Mitochondria die and turn over. Mutations accumulate. "This creates an aging clock that progressively erodes our energetic capacity until there is insufficient energy flow for optimal tissue function, at which point symptoms ensue…As the severity of the energy defect increases, more systems become affected until death ensues." (Wallace, 2011)

- "The higher the mitochondrial content per gram of muscle, the lower the rate of respiration required per mitochondrion for any given workload." (Hood, 2001) An increase in the number of mitochondria leads to a decrease in oxidation by free radicals in the muscles during intense exercise due to a decrease in production of ROS in the mitochondria. (Boveris & Chance, 1973; Davies et al., 1981; Jenkins et al., 1983)

- "Numerous randomized studies have, in general, failed to demonstrate a benefit from antioxidant therapy and large meta-analysis studies suggests that in some cases, certain antioxidants may actually increase mortality…it is possible that the hint that antioxidants might increase cancer incidence may be a result of the ability of antioxidants to protect genetically damaged precancerous cells from undergoing apoptosis. Nonetheless, it is also possible that chronic low dose antioxidants inhibit the normal hormetic response and therefore block the induction of a broad array of cytoprotective measures the organism would normally undertake." (Yun & Finkel, 2014)

  "Consistent with the concept of mitohormesis, exercise-induced oxidative stress ameliorates insulin resistance and causes an adaptive response promoting endogenous antioxidant defense capacity. Supplementation with antioxidants may preclude these health-promoting effects of exercise in humans." (Ristow et al., 2009)

"Antioxidant supplementation does not offer protection against exercise-induced lipid peroxidation and inflammation and may hinder the recovery of muscle damage." (Teixeira et al., 2009)

- "ROS-defenses are severely undermined in structurally compromised mitochondria…and that turns mitochondria into net producers of ROS…Intact mitochondria serve as a net sink rather than a net source of ROS." (Andreyev et al., 2004)

Part II: The Ferocity of Life

A Long and Winding Road

- "Endurance traditionally has been associated with the necessity to fight fatigue and with increasing the athlete's organism's tolerance to unfavorable changes in the internal environment. It was thought that endurance is developed only when athletes reached the desired degrees of fatigue…Such views linked endurance to a fatalistically inevitable decrease in work capacity…and lead to a passive attitude towards endurance development…'tolerate' and put up with the unavoidable unpleasant sensations rather than actively search for training means that reduce fatigue, postpone it, and make it less severe.

  "[Yet] the goal is not taking the athlete to exhaustion to accustom him to metabolic acidosis, as it is often understood in athletic practice, but just the opposite…to develop alactic power and to couple it with oxidative phosphorylation.

  "…To be even more laconic, training must have an "anti-glycolytic" direction, that is lower glycolysis involvement to an absolute possible minimum." (Verkhoshansky, 1988)

The Three Energy Systems

- The approximate contribution of the three main energy systems to the total energy output in brief and all-out dynamic exercise graph is largely based on high-level athletes' veloergometer data. (Volkov & Yaruzhny, 1984; Volkov et al., 2000)

  The limitations of such a generalized graph become apparent once we consider the following data from what appears to be a highly homogenous group, the Finnish national team 100-meter sprinters. After a 40-meter sprint, less than five seconds, the slower ones (even though they were all sub-11 seconds) depleted nearly 43 percent of their CP and the faster ones around 63 percent. (Hirvonen et al., 1987)

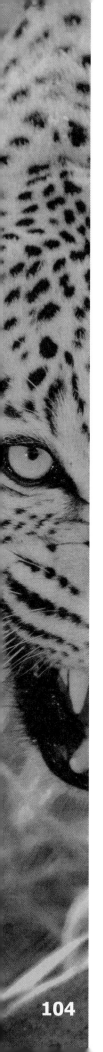

This is just one of the many reasons why there are so many conflicting timelines of the energy systems' contribution in the literature.

Nevertheless, to advance program design, generalize we must. And then, when necessary, individualize.

- Since the rate of CP breakdown is modulated by the CP/Cr ratio, the ATP output of the creatine kinase reaction drops long before the CP is exhausted. (Sahlin, 2006)

The Emergency System

- Quote. (Yakovlev, 1983)

- The myokinase reaction takes place in muscles in conditions of pronounced muscular fatigue, when the rate of ATP resynthesis no longer balances out the rate of ATP hydrolysis and there is a significant increase in ADP concentration. The MK reaction is easily reversible. (Volkov et al., 2000)

- The myokinase reaction is observed in all-out sprints longer than 10–15 seconds. (Spriet, 2006)

Intensity is Not the Effort, but the Output

- Products of ATP hydrolysis induce synthesis of mitochondrial proteins on the genetic level. (Meerson, 1971)

- AMPK is the "master switch" that triggers MT biogenesis in fast-twitch fibers. AMPK controls PGC-1α and mitochondrial enzyme gene expression in skeletal muscle. (Jäger et al., 2007) AMPK is a low cellular energy sensor that measures the AMP/ATP ratio, so on the cellular level, it is activated by a high AMP/ATP ratio. (Gowans & Hardie, 2014)

- 100 percent intensity represents MAP. (Selouyanov, 1991) "Maximum Anaerobic Power (MAP)…[is] the ability to effectively execute short-term (10–15 seconds) anaerobic work at the maximum level of power output." (Verkhoshansky, 2011)

- "If exercise…intensity falls low enough that glycolysis or the aerobic system can match energy consumption rates, then the cellular concentration of ATP will increase." (Stone et al., 2007)

Muscular ATP balance disruption starts taking place at different intensities, depending on the athlete's level. (Yakovlev, 1974) All athletes, from beginners to Masters of Sport, experience serious disruption of ATP balance in their muscles when running 100–400 meters in competition, but not at longer distances, with the exception of low-level athletes who experience it at 800 meters as well. (Krasnova et al., 1972)

Note the CP mechanism's contribution at the above distances and 800 meters:

Relative contribution of different energy systems to competition sprinting and running, % (Volkov et al., 2000)			
	CP	Glycolysis	Aerobic
100m	50	50	—
200m	25	65	10
400m	12.5	62.5	25
800m	Minimal	50	50

- There is a linear relationship between the exercise intensity and the rate of CP depletion. (Volkov et al., 2000)

...And Then the Wheels Come Off

- A single Wingate long sprint strongly activates AMPD (Bogdanis et al., 1995; Esbjörnsson-Liljedahl et al., 1985; Hargreaves et al., 1998); resting plasma ammonia concentration six minutes after a Wingate test reached 441 percent of the base level (Bogdanis et al., 1995). Thus, even though a single Wingate sprint increases the AMP/ATP ratio by as much as 21 times (Morales-Alamo et al., 2013), we consider the 30-second duration excessive and inefficient.

- "Mammalian skeletal muscle has evolved to minimize the loss of ATP to IMP and IMP to inosine and hypoxanthine during exercise and recovery from exercise, as IMP resynthesis requires de novo synthesis of the adenine nucleotides, which takes some time. For example, other species (fish) will degrade all of the ATP stored in the muscle to IMP through the above reactions and much of the IMP to its degradation products in an extreme, life-threatening sprint situation. (Pearson et al., 1990) These animals then require six to twelve hours to regenerate the adenosine backbone in order to return to the resting concentration of ATP to normal." (Hargreaves, 2006)

- "[In silico] CFS simulations exhibit critically low levels of ATP, where an increased rate of cell death would be expected. To stabilize the energy supply at low ATP concentrations the total adenine nucleotide pool is reduced substantially causing a prolonged recovery time even without consideration of other factors, such as immunological dysregulations and oxidative stress. Repeated exercises worsen this situation considerably. Furthermore, CFS simulations exhibited an increased acidosis and lactate accumulation consistent with experimental observations." (Lengert & Drossel, 2015)

- There appears to be a strong correlation between blood lactate and ammonia in brief intense exercise. Goldman & Lowenstein (1977) concluded that the purine nucleotide cycle in skeletal muscles operates under the conditions "associated with an increased rate of glycolysis." In both trained sprinters and long distance runners, there is a significant relationship between peak blood ammonia and lactate after supramaximal veloergometer exercise. (Itoh & Ohkuwa, 1990)

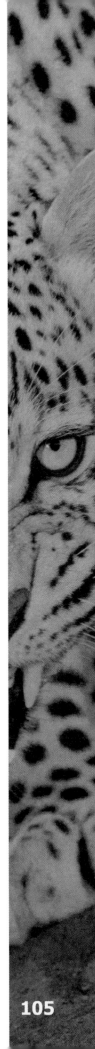

There was a sharp increase in adenine nucleotide pool degradation in untrained subjects in treadmill exercise when the BLa reached around 9mM. "The data further support the hypothesis that there is a critical intramuscular pH below which there is a stimulus to AN degradation during intense exercise, possibly as a result of a substantial reduction in the kinetics of adenosine diphosphate (ADP) rephosphorylation provided by phosphocreatine, resulting in an increase in [ADP]." (Sewell et al., 1994)

In elite 400-meter sprinters and hurdlers, blood lactate and ammonia displayed a strong correlation. (Gorostiaga et al., 2010) The researchers stressed that when the blood lactate levels do not exceed 8–12mM, the muscles' energy status and maximal running velocity or muscle generating capacity are maintained—while higher levels decrease all of the above and delay functional recovery.

- In all-out dynamic exercise muscle [La] barely rises above the resting levels for the first five seconds. Then lactate concentration approximately doubles from five to 10 seconds, from 10 seconds to 20, from 20 seconds to 30, and from 30 seconds to 60. (Volkov et al., 2000)

- In trained athletes muscular activity produces significantly less deamination byproduct IMP and more ADP and AMP than in untrained people. (Yakovlev, 1971) Among the adaptations to exercise is reduced deamination of AMP and ADP. (Yakovlev, 1974) Overtraining lowers one's resistance to deamination. (Yakovlev, 1974)

Sweet Spot in Time

- The critical CP capacity, below which a high rate of ATP resynthesis is impossible, is about a third of the total alactic capacity. (Volkov et al., 2000)

- Women, trained or untrained, produce less lactic acid than men in the same category. (Kotz, 1998) After supramaximal exercise women exhibit lower peak blood ammonia than men. (Itoh & Ohkuwa, 1993) Women junior rowers produced significantly less ammonia than men. No correlation was found between the active muscle mass and blood ammonia levels. Two explanations were suggested: a lower ratio of fast-twitch fibers or a lower AMPD activity in women than in men. (Lutoslawska et al., 1992)

Myokinase in white fibers is more active than in slow fibers (Kleine & Chlond, 1966; Raggi et al., 1969) and so is AMPD (Raggi et al., 1969). Muscles with a low mitochondria count produce more ammonia than mitochondria rich muscles. (Gerez & Kirsten, 1965) Not surprisingly, sprinters produce significantly more ammonia in supramaximal exercise than long-distance runners. (Itoh & Ohkuwa, 1990) Well-trained male judoka exhibited peak ammonia value in blood after just 15 seconds of all-out veloergometer exercise. (Itoh & Ohkuwa, 1991)

After a 75-meter sprint, 14- to 16-year-old prospective male sprinters registered significantly higher levels of blood ammonia than prospective middle-distance runners of the same age and gender. (Hageloch et al., 1990)

- Based on the available research, we conclude that the magnitude of AMP accumulation is determined by the difference between the rate of ATP hydrolysis and ATP rephosphorylation, minus the AMP removed through deamination and propose a formula:

$$[AMP] = ((\Delta \text{ ATP hydrolysis} - \Delta \text{ ATP rephosphorylation}) : \Delta \text{ } t) - [AMP] \text{ removed through deamination}$$

10x10, RELOADED

- Rest intervals of no less than two-and-a-half to three minutes are needed between 10- to 15-second bouts of maximal intensity dynamic exercise repeats. Typically, eight to 10 such bouts may be done with such rest periods before the CP concentration reaches its critical value and the power sharply declines. (Volkov et al., 2000)

- CP recovery is biphasic, with a steep initial phase about three minutes long that is followed by a slow phase. (Sahlin et al., 1979) Full CP recovery after intense exercise typically takes five to eight minutes. (Volkov et al., 2000)

- In the Soviet weightlifting methodology a maximal training volume per exercise per training session was about 100 repetitions for experienced lifters. (Tsatsouline, 2014, based on many sources. See Plan Strong™ for references.)

- Quotes. (Vorobyev, 1989)

THE MELODY IS IN THE RESTS

- In addition to the AMP/ATP ratio, the CP/Cr ratio is another important AMPK regulator, with the higher ratios inhibiting AMPK in a dose-dependent manner and lower ratios activating it. (Ponticos et al., 1998) Viollet et al. (2010) even proposed that in brief intense exercise, the dropping [CP], rather than an increase in [AMP], may be the key regulator of AMPK.

  It may be the rate, rather than the magnitude, of fuel depletion that increases AMPK activity. (Clark et al., 2004) Most likely, both have an effect: "AMPK is activated in…human muscle during cycle exercise in a time and exercise-intensity-dependent manner." (Jørgensen et al., 2006)

- Rest intervals classification. (Matveev, 1991)

A RUGBY LESSON

- Repeat sprint ability research. (Balsom et al., 1992a, b; Dawson et al., 1996; Dawson, 1998; Volkov et al., 2000)

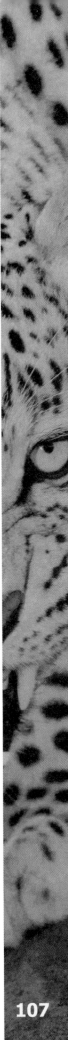

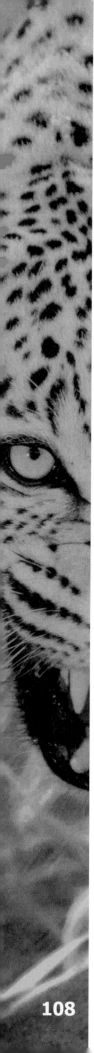

- After five six-second velo sprints done every 30 seconds, the peak power is down by only eight to 10 percent. (Morin et al., 2011) Contrast: The same 30 seconds of velo sprinting done all at once reduces the power five times more—by 40–50 percent. (Nevill et al., 1996)

  Dawson et al. (1996) proposed five six-second sprints done every 30 seconds with active recovery between sprints as an effective training series for athletes whose sports demand repeated sprinting. They point out that if the athlete did more, he would be starting the sixth sprint with less than half of the pre-exercise level CP (45 percent). They argue that the subsequent sets would unavoidably be relying less on the CP pathway and more on glycolysis and oxidative phosphorylation.

  The argument to limit a series of short sprints to around 30 seconds of total work is also supported by the results of Gaitanos et al. (1993) and Mendez-Villanueva et al. (2012). Both studied 10 six-second sprints with 30 seconds rest. In the former study, the PPO decreased by 15.9 percent after five sprints and by 33.4 percent after 10. The MPO decreased by 12.6 percent and 26.6 percent, respectively. Mendez-Villanueva et al. (2012) recorded similar dynamics.

- There is a linear relationship between the exercise intensity and the rate of CP depletion. (Volkov et al., 2000)

- After five six-second sprints done every 30 seconds, the CP was down to 27.4 percent of the base level. (Dawson et al., 1996) Since these measurements were taken 10 seconds post-exercise and the CK reaction is most rapid in the beginning of CP recovery, one could speculate that the magnitude of CP depletion was greater than 75 percent.

  In addition, 10 seconds after five six-second sprints done every 30 seconds, ATP was down to 66.2 percent of the base level (Dawson et al., 1996), which is a high magnitude of depletion for this substrate, based on the fact that ATP is very well protected and after all-out sprints or repeated sprints the ATP concentration decreases only by around 20–40 percent below its resting level. (Bogdanis et al., 1996; Hargreaves et al., 1998; Jones et al., 1985; Parolin et al., 1999; Spriet et al., 1989) Therefore, additional sprints are not likely to deplete ATP any more.

- Advanced Iranian wrestlers' study. (Farzad et al., 2011)

The Finishing Touches

- The work-to-rest ratio for alactic interval training. (Fox & Matthews, 1974)

- Recommendations in literature on the volume of exercise targeting the phosphagen system vary greatly, e.g., from below two-and-a-half minutes per session (Tabarchouk et al., 2014) to greater than 10 minutes (Matveev, 1991). We chose the number of two-and-a-half minutes, which happens to correspond to Volkov's maximal volume for about 15-second alactic capacity repeats.

- Rest between series of RSA sprints must be greater than three minutes. (Volkov et al., 2000). Dawson et al. (1996) found three minutes insufficient to fully replenish the CP stores and suggested resting longer between such series, "perhaps for four to six minutes."

Part III: The Power Drills

The Power Drills of Choice

- Quote about "actively accelerated ballistics." (Verkhoshansky & Siff, 2009)

The Pushup: A Classic, Remastered

- Quote. (Zatsiorsky, 1966)

- Power is typically trained with 40–70 percent of maximal resistance. (Volkov et al., 2000)

Part IV: Happy Hunting!

Where Is the Cardio?

- Quote. (Yakovlev, 1974)

- The cardiac output of an untrained adult is sufficient to supply oxygen for running long distance at a Master of Sport level. The bottleneck is the lack of mitochondrial development in skeletal muscles. As a result, the forming H^+ causes muscular fatigue and stresses the cardiorespiratory system with nonmetabolic CO_2. (Antonov, 2013)

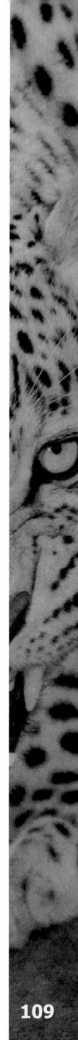

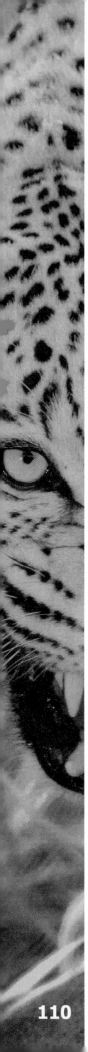

- "Perfecting endurance was seen primarily as increasing the VO_2 max, since it was believed that this criterion offers a generalized assessment of the development level of the physiological functions responsible for intake, transport, and utilization of oxygen in the organism. And in spite of the appearance of extensive experimental data witnessing that in the competition season the VO_2 max decreases, as a rule, and that athletes with different (and even rather modest) VO_2 max can post high results, and that, finally, in the last decades the growth of athletic achievements has not been accompanied by a VO_2 max increase in top athletes (Verkhoshansky, 1985), the faith in vegetative preparedness as the main factor determining endurance has not been shaken." (Verkhoshansky, 1988)

"…data indicate that an increase in endurance is related not so much with getting more oxygen in the blood and improving its transport to the working muscle as with an increase in these muscles' ability to utilize a higher percentage of oxygen. Therefore it is not the VO_2 max value but the intra-muscular factors governed by the adaptation of the muscular apparatus to prolonged strenuous work that determine the athlete's endurance level.

"Thus endurance development is related not only to perfecting the "respiratory" abilities but also to…an increase in the skeletal muscles' strength and oxidizing properties. Therefore, the main direction in endurance development must not be a 'habituation' to a high level of lactate in blood but a pursuit to lower the share of glycolysis in supplying work and perfecting the muscles' capability to oxidize lactate in the course of exercise. In other words, endurance development must be oriented primarily at the elimination of the discrepancy between the muscles' glycolytic and oxidizing capabilities, which happens to be the main cause of high lactate concentration, and at a maximal utilization of the aerobic energy pathway." (Verkhoshansky, 1985)

THE DELTA 20 PRINCIPLE

- Quote. (Vorobyev, 1977)

- Quote. (Vorobyev, 1989)

- *Stable structural constants.* (Chernyak, 1978)

BUILT TO LAST

- In detraining, the first adaptations lost are those related to the functional condition of the vegetative systems (VO_2 max, stroke volume, etc.). (Yakovlev, 1974)

- The higher the athlete's VO_2 max, the steeper the detraining curve. (Platonov et al., 2004)

- The cardiac adaptations to interval training are not stable—in contrast with the steady effort method. (Platonov et al., 2004)

- Morphological adaptations are more stable than biochemical adaptations. (Yakovlev, 1974)

While cytoplasm-based enzymes are unstable (Yakovlev, 1974), dehydrogenases' activity stays up at a trained level for a long time (Yakovlev, 1950).

Training residuals after stopping concentrated loading (Issurin & Shklyar, 2002)		
Quality	Residuals' duration, days	Underlying mechanisms
Aerobic endurance	30 ± 5	Aerobic enzymes, MT mass, capillaries, hemoglobin, glycogen, higher rate of lipolysis
Maximal strength	30 ± 5	Neural and hypertrophy
Anaerobic glycolytic endurance	18 ± 4	Glycolytic enzymes, glycogen, buffering capacity, higher lactic acid tolerance
Alactic maximal speed	5 ± 3	Neural, CP storage

- The longer the training, the deeper the adaptation caused by it and the longer it remains in detraining. For example, if the training lasted 30 days, 30 days after stopping training, the glycogen and CP content and the phosphorylation activity of muscle tissues reduce to pre-training levels. If the training lasted 90 days, 30 days after cessation of training glycogen and phosphorylation activity did not decrease at all and CP content, while it went down, it did not return to pre-training levels. (Yampolskaya & Yakovlev, 1951)

- The greater the speed component in low-volume maintenance loads, the more pronounced their detraining prevention effects. (Yampolskaya & Yakovlev, 1951)

- Quote. (Yakovlev, 1974)

- The greater the training frequency, the more rapid the detraining and vice versa. (Hettinger, 1961)

- While after exhausting running, myofibrillar protein synthesis is depressed for several days, sarcoplasmic protein synthesis accelerates right after training. (Nekrasov, 1982; Séne, 1987) This suggests that one can effectively train the mitochondria daily. (Myakinchenko & Selouyanov, 2005)

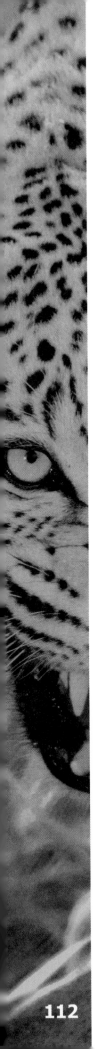

THE SCHEDULE

- A correct warm-up significantly increases performance in power exercises. (Verkhoshansky, 1977) "A warm-up does not have a statistically significant positive effect on strength." (Kotz, 1998)

- Quote. (Verkhoshansky and Siff, 2009)

EACH CHOOSES FOR ONESELF

- High load variability postpones plateaus. (Vorobyev, 1977)

- Training on the far right of the force-velocity curve (speed) has a carryover to the middle of the curve (power). (Khokhmut, 1962)

- Quickness and frequency of unloaded movements are developed with 15–20 percent of maximal resistance. (Verkhoshansky, 1988)

- Early Soviet coaching was driven by Pavlov's teaching that one adapts best "when certain stimuli are repeated in a strict order and with strict intervals between them." (Pavlov, 1949) In the 1960s, high regularity of training was still considered an asset. (Luchkin, 1962) Later, it was concluded that while a "Monday/Wednesday/Friday" type rhythm is appropriate for beginners, it is suboptimal for experienced athletes who need more variability, at least outside the competition period. (Vorobyev, 1977)

- Quote. (Roman, 1986)

- In developing aerobic endurance and muscle mass, load variability is limited. When training goals are speed-strength or strength without increasing mass, variability is greater. (Zakharov et al., 1994)

STRONG ENDURANCE™ Seminar

Learn how to build a race car—with a hybrid's fuel economy

Russian coach Andrey Kozhurkin made a 50,000-foot observation on the two diametrically opposed philosophies of stimulating adaptation.

The traditional one is pushing to the limit: "What does not kill me, makes me stronger."

The alternative is to train to "avoid (or at least delay) the unfavorable internal conditions… that lead to failure" or reduced performance.

Let us use strength training as an example. The majority of bodybuilders and recreational athletes use the first approach. They train to failure.

In contrast, strength athletes such as Olympic weightlifters and powerlifters follow the second approach. 1,000-pound squatter Dr. Fred Hatfield famously proclaimed that one ought to "train to success," as opposed to failure. The differences between the American and Russian powerlifting methodologies notwithstanding, both countries' strength elites share the same conviction that failure is not an option.

In endurance training the first philosophy represents the consensus. Coaches expose athletes to acid baths to improve buffering. This is what Arthur Jones from Nautilus called "metabolic conditioning" back in 1975.

We shall go the other way: *anti-glycolytic training.*

This revolutionary method has delivered performance breakthroughs on a number of Russian national teams in a mind numbingly diverse array of sports: judo, cross country skiing, rowing, bicycle racing, full contact karate…

The Quick & the Dead protocol is just the tip of the anti-glycolytic training iceberg—and only one of the eighteen state of the art training templates you will learn at the Strong Endurance™ seminar:

✓ **Templates #1-7: Fast and Intermediate Fibers' Aerobic Training**
Make your fast fibers aerobic—without sacrificing power and strength—for games and combat sports.

✓ **Templates #8-11: Intermediate Fibers' Aerobic Training**
For military, law enforcement, first responders.

✓ **Templates #12-13: Intermediate & Slow Fibers' Aerobic Training**
March or die. Lose fat.

✓ **Templates #14-16: Fast and Intermediate Fibers' Hypertrophy**
Build more muscle—while improving your acid buffering.

✓ **Templates #17-18: Slow Fibers' Hypertrophy**
A game changer for wrestling and for training around injuries.

To give you an idea of what else you will learn, here is the table of contents of the dense, heavily referenced Strong Endurance™ seminar manual:

TABLE OF CONTENTS

Journeys of energy: summaries of key reactions...1
Stress & adaptation..3
    Stress...3
    "The cost of adaptation"...5
    Stress free adaptation...6
Mitochondria: "Masters of life and death"...13
    Big picture...13
    Reactive oxygen species (ROS) and peroxidation of lipids (POL)...............14
    Damage by ROS/POL..15
    Acidosis promotes ROS/POL...16
    Yet infrequent glycolytic exercise may be advisable.....................................17
    Benefits of ROS..17
    Defenses against ROS...18
    How to build mitochondria with exercise..18
Endurance, 50,000'..21
VO₂max, 30,000-50,000'...23
    VO₂max is not the end-all..24
    How to increase VO₂max with steady state exercise....................................25
    How to increase VO₂max with German interval training..............................27
    Classic interval training vs. "HIIT"..29
    Redlining the heart rate is dangerous..30
    Vascular adaptations..31
    "Grinds" are not optimal for "cardio"..33
Anti-glycolytic training..35
    Acidosis severely limits performance..35
    The birth and philosophy of AGT..37
    AGT Swedish forerunner..40
    Aerobic advantage...49
    How to make fast twitch fibers aerobic—the classic Soviet model...............50
    Mitochondrial quantity vs. quality...52
    Soviet and Russian experimental anti-glycolytic research.............................54
    Soviet and Russian AGT protocols...66
    AGT load variability...70

Anti-glycolytic, StrongFirst®...75
Glycolytic peaking..89
    Glycolytic training: for the competition period only....................................89
    Select glycolytic peaking tactics..92
Strength [for] endurance..99
[Para] static endurance..103
Planning..107
    Balance of qualities...107
    Long(er) term..107
    Month...111
    Week: load and recovery...112
    Week: balance of qualities...114
    Week: schedules...116
    Session: load..117
    Session: effort...120
    Session: specificity and variability...123
    Session: modalities..126
    Session: fatigue and recovery..127
AGT templates & plans...131
    Templates..132
    Plans..144
        019: 5min S&S one-arm swing (template #1 + peaking).................144
        020: 5min S&S one-arm swing (template #1 + peaking).................149
        260, 360: 5min S&S one-arm swing (template #1 +"2:2" peaking)...151
        033D: swing + pushup (template #2)..153
        044C: snatch (template #2)..159
        044B: snatch (template #2)..162
        1050: long cycle C&J (~template #2)...164
        551: long cycle C&J (template #3)..165
        523A: TSC snatch (template #4)..166
        524A: SFG snatch (template #4)...167
        060: snatch (template #10)..169
        550: long cycle C&J (template #5)..172
        133: push + pull (template #16)..173

The seminar is taught both in plain English and in biochemistry terms.

Learn how to build a race car—with a hybrid's fuel economy.

StrongFirst.com/special-events/strong-endurance/